Communication Options in the
Education of Deaf Children

Communication Options in the Education of Deaf Children

Wendy Lynas

W

Whurr Publishers Ltd
London

© 1994 Whurr Publishers Ltd

First published 1994 by
Whurr Publishers Ltd
19b Compton Terrace, London N1 2UN, England

Reprinted 1995, 1999 and 2004

British Library Cataloguing-in-Publication Data
A catalogue record for this book is available from the
British Library

ISBN 1-897635-41-9

Contents

Preface

A few years ago some colleagues and myself in the Department of Audiology, Education of the Deaf and Speech Pathology at The University of Manchester entered the communication debate in deaf education by examining the challenge being made to Oralism by Total Communication. We published a booklet* which reflected a serious concern that enthusiasm for TC was not matched by language benefits for deaf children and young people being taught by the TC method. This concern about the efficacy of TC has now come to be shared not only by oralists – ever faithful to the idea that deaf children could, and therefore should, be taught to talk through talk – but also by the recently emerged Bilingualists who believe that deaf children can acquire language in a normal manner only through what is held to be 'their own' language, sign language.

In writing this book my intention is to engage in the contemporary, and now broadened communication debate, and to try to make a useful and dispassionate contribution to it. There is, I feel, a need to re-evaluate and reappraise the arguments and evidence for different approaches in the education of deaf children, and to see how things stand at present. Even a brief glance at this fascinating scene gives cause for concern in that it reveals not so much a debate as a partisan war. I do not, however, want just to satisfy a self-indulgent curiosity: I want to do my best to offer the variety of professionals who serve deaf children – teachers, educational psychologists, speech therapists, etc. – a reasoned examination of the various approaches currently advocated. I am concerned that those who have to make decisions about communication options, and those who have to put these decisions into practice, are as aware as they possibly can be about the implications of the different communication practices currently on offer. I am particularly concerned that the parents of deaf children are equipped to make

*Lynas, Huntington and Tucker (1988). *A Critical Examination of Different Approaches to Communication in the Education of Deaf Children*, The Ewing Foundation.

sense and meaning of the conflicting views they hear advocated and of the possibly contradictory advice they receive.

Decisions made for young deaf children can be fateful for their life chances so I make a strong plea to anyone who has a part to play in the decisions so crucially affecting the lives of these young persons to be objective and not to be swayed by appealing but superficial arguments. Everyone must be on guard against being beguiled by ideologies and policies simply because they happen to be fashionable.

There are no absolutely clear solutions to the problem of giving deaf children communication and language nor of providing them with educational opportunities equal to those of their hearing peers. There is no certain way of knowing how future deaf adults will want to live their lives. Unfortunately, deaf children are not in a position to make their own decisions about these crucial matters. It is present-day adults who must make the decisions on behalf of deaf children and it is they, I suggest, who have a moral duty to get to *know as much as possible* about the nature and implications of available communication approaches.

I offer this book to provide knowledge and awareness to all those who are concerned about the education of deaf children. I cannot claim that the book provides easy answers but I have done what I can to air the problems and put them on display.

I would like to express my sincere appreciation to those friends and colleagues who have done so many useful things to support my writing. I have received encouragement and moral support, ideas, facts, advice about style and organisation of the book and help with the more tedious and tricky aspects of word-processing, from several people who already had much else to do with their time. Many, many thanks.

Wendy Lynas
Centre for Audiology, Education of the Deaf and Speech Pathology
The University of Manchester
Manchester, UK.
June 1994

Chapter 1
Introduction

Human communication depends, for the most part, on language and language in turn facilitates socialisation and access to the cultural knowledge of the wider society. Indeed, it is language itself which is the repository of human cultural knowledge. It is through the medium of language that a person can become a fully socialised, integrated human being.

For most people the language preferred as a means of human communication is speech – an auditory-oral system of language. It is speech itself which is the medium through which verbal language is acquired in the first place.

In using language we are involved in processes which are amongst the most complex of human activity though we are largely unaware of what is going on in our brains to produce it. When we communicate through language we order our words according to intricate rules of syntax. In our speech we observe rules of rhythm, stress and intonation so as to communicate effectively. When we speak we rapidly and usually unreflectingly select from a vocabulary of around 50 000 words (Newell and Simon, 1972) at a rate of five selections a second (Bench, 1992). There is probably no other human activity which requires such a high decision rate of such complexity yet we accomplish the task so readily we are largely unaware that we are making decisions. In talking with others we follow rules of conversation and observe rules of interpersonal interaction attuned to the social context, rules which we take for granted because exposure to the language culture has, over time, built them into our heads in fine detail. We almost certainly could not specify all the rules governing our communicative behaviour yet we seem to have some internal mechanisms for putting the rules of language and communication into operation so that, on the whole, we can communicate effectively.

Deafness from birth, however, imposes a severe threat to the development of verbal language and communication. The deaf* child has the normal human capacity and potential to assimilate language and to

*Since the focus of this work is on children with substantial hearing losses, the term 'deaf' is used rather than 'hearing-impaired'. It also has the advantage of being a shorter term!

1

develop all the complex rules of language and communication through culturally mediated contact with other human beings. He or she is potentially just the same as any child in this and other respects but can be prevented from realising that potential if the vital link of hearing, which normally triggers that development through access to the speech of others, is missing. Language, which is acquired without much conscious effort or struggle by a child with normal hearing, during the early years of life, can become an elusive goal for many young deaf children and without language, access to wider cultural socialization and education becomes difficult. Without the development of language a deaf child's – indeed any child's – fulfilment as a social human being is seriously jeopardised. Because deafness from birth is potentially so fatefully consequential everyone involved with the care, development and education of deaf children has, as their prime interest, a concern to activate the language capacities within the deaf child so as to enable linguistic development in all its full complexity. Everyone wants for the deaf child an easy and fluent system of communication so that relationships with other people can be rich and varied. With language, literacy can be acquired and all agree that literacy is a major goal of deaf education to enable access for deaf individuals to the vast store of human knowledge which is available through the written word.

There is also general agreement that deaf children should have full access to a broad and balanced curriculum during their school years and that deaf children should have an equal opportunity to develop their full potential as members of society. But *how* to unlock the barrier to language which deafness represents and *how* to trigger the language facility of the brain to ensure for the developing deaf individual free and fluent communication is, and always has been the subject of much controversy – controversy which is currently accompanied by a great deal of heated emotion and heavy rhetoric. Traditionally, at the extremes of the controversy are 'oralists', who believe that deaf children should be given speech and speech alone, and 'manualists', who believe that deaf children should communicate only through sign. The dichotomy between the two positions has, over recent times, become less clear-cut as the issues concerning language acquisition have come to be perceived as more complex than previously thought. There is today, perhaps more than ever before, a greater variety of views about the type of language deaf children should acquire and the communication means by which language should be established. A newcomer to the scene, such as the parent of a newly diagnosed deaf child, or a student-teacher of the deaf, is likely to be bewildered and confused by the conflicting viewpoints as to what is best for the deaf child with respect to language acquisition and mode of communication. So, a brief foreword concerning the historical background to the current communication debate is appropriate in this *Introduction*.

An examination of communication approaches used in deaf education over the centuries reveals 'swings of the pendulum' with oralism gaining favour at certain times and pure signing gaining ascendancy at other times. For most of the twentieth century the Western world has been dominated by the 'oral' approach which followed from the 'Viva la Parola' resolution passed at the first major international conference on deaf education, held in Milan, 1880. The popularity of oralism was reinforced by the emergence of the new 'science' of audiology and technological developments in measurement and aiding of hearing. The relative prosperity of industrial countries during the post-war period was associated with an expansion of special educational provision and improved facilities for deaf children (Watson, 1967; Connor, 1986). The special school system offered small classes, highly qualified specialist teachers, audiologists and modern amplification equipment. It was optimistically believed that, through the use of specialist techniques and equipment and more individual attention, deaf children would be afforded the same educational opportunity and the same broad curriculum as was available to schoolchildren everywhere. The explicit aim of oral special schools was to teach deaf children to talk and to develop literacy so that their achievements would be similar to those achieved by the school population as a whole (Ewing and Ewing, 1961).

However, during the 1960s considerable concern developed about the standards that were being achieved in schools for the deaf. In the USA a special Committee, the Babbidge Committee, was established to investigate the educational attainments of deaf children in America (Babbidge, 1965). The Babbidge Committee reported that, overall, deaf children were achieving very low standards of literacy and educational attainment and it questioned the continued use of oral-only approaches. According to Schlesinger (1986), referring to North America in the 1960s:

> Publications lamenting the achievement of deaf school children multiplied. A number of educators of the deaf, a number of psychologists and psychiatrists, (most of whom were well acquainted with minority status), and an even larger proportion of deaf adults remained puzzled about the fervent disdain shown toward the use of sign, and began to more openly advocate its use (p. 89).

The supremacy of oralism was similarly challenged in the UK with the establishment of the Lewis Committee whose terms of reference were: 'To consider the place, if any, of finger spelling and signing in the education of the deaf' (DES, 1968). The Lewis Committee reported a survey of attainments of 270 children with pre-lingual hearing losses of 70 dB or more, born in 1947, who in 1962–3 were attending special schools for the deaf. Of these young people:

only 11.6 per cent had clear intelligible speech and good lipreading ability making it relatively easy for the interviewer to communicate with them by speech (DES, 1968, pp. 12–13).

Though supporting more research, 'to determine whether or not and in what circumstances the introduction of manual media of communication would lead to improvement in the education of deaf children', the Lewis Committee did not make any firm recommendations to abandon oralism or introduce sign. However, a subsequent survey undertaken in England and Wales during the early 1970s confirmed the persistence of low standards in deaf education and produced an explicit challenge to the perpetuation of an oral-only approach (Conrad, 1979). Conrad's survey revealed that the average reading age on leaving school of those with average hearing losses greater than 85 dB HL (n=205), was below 9 years. Fifty per cent were judged to be totally illiterate. Nearly three-quarters of the sample had speech which was 'unintelligible' or 'very hard to understand'. In the light of the evidence Conrad (1979) was led to the conclusion that:

> we are confronted here with an inflexible chain between deafness and oral language which continues to defy technological assault (p. 241).

In short, during the late 1960s and early 1970s the oralist position became more vulnerable and advocacy of signing more insistent. In North America and in parts of Europe, (for example, in Scandinavia) there was a fairly dramatic switch in communication approaches for deaf children, that is for children with severe to profound and profound hearing losses** (Schlesinger, 1986), after which only 'pockets of oralism' remained. Total Communication, the method of using signs with speech, was introduced in the belief that this would improve communication and accelerate verbal language development. The formal introduction of signing in the education of deaf children in the UK and some parts of Europe was clearly evident but not as widespread as in North America and Scandinavia. In the UK there remained a significant number of educators who were not convinced that introducing signs would 'improve matters' for the majority of deaf children.

The communication debate during the 1970s and early 1980s was largely between 'oralism' and 'TC': oralists felt the need to defend their position with greater emphasis and clarity, whereas advocates of TC believed their method to be 'the way forward'. However, during the 1980s a new position, which came to be termed 'bilingualism', emerged

---

**A severe hearing loss has been defined as an average loss in the better ear which exceeds 70 dB; a profound hearing loss is an average loss in the better ear which exceeds 95 dB (BATOD, 1981). Oralists emphasise that total deafness in young children is extremely rare, and oralists do not make firm demarcations between levels or categories of hearing loss. For most oralists, all deaf children have residual hearing which can be used for the development of speech.

as a critique of both oralism and TC. It arose in part from the greater acceptance of signs in the education of deaf children and in part from the developing voice of the deaf signing adult population. Bilingualism accords a much more positive and central role to sign language as a source of language and as a means of education for deaf children: it challenges the principle held both within oralism and TC of the primacy of verbal language as the first language of deaf children.

Currently, the debate is broadly three-way: oralists believe that speech is accessible to deaf children and that language is best acquired through the spoken word; advocates of TC judge that significant numbers of deaf children need the support of signs if they are to develop verbal language; bilingualists assert the right of the deaf child to sign language as a first language and as a means of social identity.

The aim of this book is to examine critically the three broad categories of communication approach which are currently advocated by the different schools of thinking concerned with the socialisation and education of deaf children: the Auditory-Oral, the Total Communication and the Bilingual. The intention is to identify the claims made for the different approaches so as to elucidate the assumptions made by each, assess the arguments they offer and present the counter-claims made by the critics of each approach. The research relating to the efficacy of each approach will be reviewed and the validity of the available evidence will be examined. The unresolved, and indeed unresolvable, ideological and political features of the debate will also be discussed and, hopefully, clarified.

The kinds of question addressed include: should every effort be made to enable the deaf child to communicate in the language which is dominant in the wider society? Can even the deafest child be enabled to receive sufficient auditory information to support the acquisition of spoken language? Is there a critical period for language learning which, if missed, leaves the deaf individual 'languageless'? Can signs be used to augment speech in the development of spoken language? Should we expect the deaf child to accommodate to the communication norms of hearing society given the difficulties involved in acquiring speech? Or, given that a substantial hearing loss represents a serious handicap in relation to spoken language, should deaf children from an early age be given the right to communicate, and indeed be educated, in a language in which they are not handicapped, namely, sign language? Should we place emphasis on the deaf child acquiring the language which belongs to the Deaf*** community and on him being 'integrated' into the hearing world as one with a distinct cultural and linguistic identity? Is it possible to get what some would call 'the best of both worlds' – can a child, deaf from

---

***'Deaf' with an upper case 'D' is now a widely accepted way of denoting cultural deafness and describes deaf people who elect to identify with the Deaf community. 'deaf' with a lower case 'd' is a broader term which can refer to anyone with a hearing loss. Not all of those who are deaf choose to be Deaf.

birth, be taught both to talk and also acquire fluency in sign language to the detriment of neither and if so at what stage of development is this possible? Can sign language be used as a means of acquiring verbal language? Can different approaches be used at different stages in a deaf child's life to the benefit of the deaf child's linguistic and educational progress?

Two fundamental issues underlie the foregoing questions. The first concerns whether or not all deaf children, however deaf, *can*, in principle and in practice, be taught to talk and understand speech. The second concerns whether or not children, however deaf, *should* be taught to talk as a first priority? The first question is concerned with what is possible and the second with what is morally desirable. There is disagreement over both types of issue, that is, disagreement on what are the appropriate goals in the education of deaf children and on what can and cannot be realistically achieved. An examination of the arguments and evidence concerning both kinds of issue does not yield easy answers. My aim is to throw light on these issues by presenting currently available information with as much clarity and as little bias as possible.

In respect of the issue of bias the author is known to have participated in the writing of a publication in support of the auditory-oral communication approach (Lynas, Huntington and Tucker, 1988). Since then, there have been developments in knowledge and thinking which make coming down firmly 'on one side or the other' all the more difficult and seemingly arrogant. However, despite the very real difficulties, the author remains, by and large, committed to the auditory-oral approach in the belief that, according to the available evidence, the auditory-oral option offers the deaf child greater opportunity and broader life-chances than either of the other two options. I will be taking this matter up in the final chapter where I shall present reasons for my continuing commitment to the auditory-oral approach.

Having expressed my personal preference, it should be emphasised that it is not my intention to proselytize. The aim is to discuss impartially and detachedly the issues and dilemmas, both practical and moral, so that readers can decide for themselves where they stand. Perhaps the major aim of this work will have been achieved if readers develop a greater sense of uncertainty about where they *do* stand. Parents and educators have ineluctably to make choices and to act but it can be of no service to deaf children if those who have to make decisions which can crucially influence the future life of the deaf individual oversimplify complex problems, ignore dilemmas, and look for easy solutions.

Chapter 2
The Auditory-Oral Approach

Modern oralists* believe that attempts should be made to *break through* the barrier to communication caused by deafness. Total deafness in children deaf from birth is extremely rare and, therefore, the overwhelming majority of profoundly deaf children have some residual hearing. Even if there is no measurable hearing at the early infant stage, it is, oralists emphasise, most unlikely that the child will have no residual hearing. It is quite commonly found that children who make no response to sound at diagnosis will show some auditory acuity at a later stage, after stimulation by hearing aids, and after some auditory experience (Tucker, 1986). Oralists believe that the residual hearing of even the deafest of children can be exploited by means of systems of amplification so that the brain receives sufficient input via the auditory channel for the development of spoken language. Oralists do not claim that normal hearing can be restored by even the best quality hearing aids, but that the spoken message, appropriately amplified, *can* provide an adequate analogue of the message received by people with normal hearing. That is to say, the auditory signals received, although filtered through the hearing loss and altered as a consequence, are believed to be sufficient to be recognised as speech signals by the brain and sufficient to allow the auditory language processing mechanisms of the brain to develop and operate.

Crucial to the modern oral approach is, therefore, that maximum use must be made of the deaf child's residual hearing. The other central principle is the provision of appropriate spoken language experience.

*The term 'oralist' is used to refer to anyone who subscribes to the auditory-oral approach. The term is an oversimplification, and the oralist position presented here in its 'pure' form would not necessarily be accepted unmodified by all those who, in broad terms, would call themselves oralists.

What is Involved in an Auditory-Oral Approach?

Provision of appropriate amplification

As soon as the infant or child is diagnosed as deaf it is considered crucially important to fit appropriate hearing aids. Without hearing aids
the child with a severe or profound hearing loss will have little or no
access to the sounds of speech. The hearing aids, therefore, must be
carefully prescribed in order to take into account the nature of the
child's hearing loss and amplification needs. Hearing aids must also be
carefully maintained so that they perform as intended. Parents, in the
first place, must take responsibility for keeping the hearing aids in
good working order and for ensuring that they are correctly placed in
the ears. This is no easy task and oralists would not deny that taking
care of the relatively small, fiddly technical devices, with parts which
can easily go wrong or break, is potentially irksome. Furthermore, to
introduce the device into an infant who resists having something
strange and possibly uncomfortable in his or her ear can compound
the difficulty. Research has demonstrated that there is a significant cor-
relation between speech achievements and good use of hearing aids
(Ling and Ling, 1978; Northcott, 1981; Markides, 1986). So despite the
difficulties involved, oralists emphasise the need for good hearing aid
use.

Since hearing aids play such a critical role in the auditory-oral
approach, oralists emphasise the need for expert and sympathetic support for parents\caregivers in the care and management of hearing aids.
In the UK, it is usual for the parents of a newly diagnosed deaf child to
receive immediate and regular support from the local peripatetic service
of teachers of the deaf.

The current oralist emphasis on the exploitation of residual hearing
through hearing aids does not imply that visual information plays no part
in the perception of speech and the understanding of spoken communication. Where there is hearing impairment the auditory sense will, so
most oralists believe, be supported by visual communication such as
facial expression, lip movements, body language, and natural gestures.
However, there is agreement among those advocating an auditory-oral
approach that the amount of *linguistic* information contained in visual
cues is limited (Clark, 1989).

Spoken language experience

The first prerequisite, then, for the development of spoken language in
the young deaf child is that the child's hearing is enhanced to the maximum by the best possible amplification. However, the matter does not
rest there: if deaf children are to develop oral language through their

hearing then there must be some oral language for them to hear. Oralists have spent a considerable amount of time thinking about how to provide the right kind of language experience during the deaf child's developing years (Nolan and Tucker, 1988; Clark, 1989).

The language learner with a profound hearing loss has the same internal language acquisition mechanisms and the same potential to construct linguistic rules as a child with normal hearing. All children need an adequate amount of language experience if they are to acquire language. If there is no language in the environment then there is no language in the child. We know this to be so from evidence of the, fortunately, rare instances of children experiencing total isolation from language during childhood (Curtiss, 1977). A profound hearing loss imposes a severe restriction on the amount of spoken language a child can experience and, therefore, developing spoken language in the deaf child is highly problematic. However, with the right quantity and quality of language input, oralists argue, the deaf child can have the necessary language experience to support oral language acquisition. We do not know *exactly* how much language input is required to supply the deaf child's language acquisition mechanisms with the requisite data (Gallaway and Woll, 1994). We do know, however, that special steps must be taken in order to ensure that the 'input', inevitably restricted by deafness, becomes, from a linguistic point of view, significant 'intake'.

Modern oralists take the view that it is very important that the spoken language surrounding the deaf child is relevant to his or her needs and interests. The language offered should be related to the child's focus of attention at any particular moment. If this is achieved the deaf child will start to perceive the auditory signals as communication symbols. This, oralists acknowledge, is not as easy as it sounds. Talking to a child who does not readily respond to communicative overtures is hard work. It is only too easy to become disheartened and not to say very much. It is also easy to talk 'over the head' of the child or to be over-directive, paying insufficient attention to what the child might be thinking or what he or she might be wanting to communicate (Gregory, Mogford and Bishop, 1979; Wood et al., 1986). Creating situations which require communicative exchange is part of the skill required by an adult in facilitating language acquisition. Observing the child closely so as to infer what the child's mind is focused on is a skill requiring patience as well as sensitivity. Whilst these skills have to be worked at by those concerned to facilitate language development in deaf children, they are not, say oralists, beyond the capacity of the 'ordinary' parent or teacher (Wood et al., 1986; Nolan and Tucker, 1988). Once adults develop a sensitivity to the deaf child's interests and communication needs, satisfying interaction can occur (Clark, 1989). The more the adult offers communication that is relevant to the deaf child's interests, the more, so it is claimed, the child will attend to speech, and the more responsive and interactive he becomes. Communicating with the deaf child gets progressively easier for the adult. And, as deaf children develop their capacity to listen, the more feedback they get from their own vocalisations and this in itself encourages further vocalisation. As the auditory signals received by the child from the spoken language environment come to be perceived as linguistic symbols so the process of language acquisition gets under way.

Once vocal communication begins it needs continuous nurturing so that the child can use his or her natural ability to infer the rules of language (Ivimey, 1977) and to acquire a vocabulary which is sufficiently rich to support his needs. The importance of maintaining a sensitive conversational approach cannot, say oralists, be emphasised enough. Keeping tuned into the deaf child's interests and using whatever language is natural to the situation is of vital importance. In this way deaf children, according to the National Aural Group:

> should absorb language by participating either receptively or expressively in communication through conversation at a level appropriate to their interests. (1981, BATOD Magazine Section).

The developing child must learn how words are used in everyday discourse: for example, he or she must be given opportunities to discover that the same words can mean different things in different contexts; that there are a number of ways of expressing a particular idea; that language can be used to express feelings, control others, make jokes, establish social contact, etc. etc. The richness and power of language is not, so it is argued, something that can be taught directly: it has to be realised through social interaction by learning how language is used in everyday life (Nolan and Tucker, 1988; Clark, 1989).

Oralists recognise that for a child with very little natural residual hearing the process of language acquisition will take longer than for a child with normal hearing (Nolan and Tucker, 1988). Most children with profound hearing losses need time to learn to listen and time to make linguistic sense of the auditory information given by the speech of others. Hence the milestones of language acquisition will not be achieved within the same timescale as with the unimpaired language learner. However, the sequence of acquisition will be similar to that of a normally hearing child and eventually, so oralists claim, the child will achieve mastery of the structure of verbal language (Clark, 1978).

Once the deaf child attends school there is an ongoing need to make demands on the child's developing linguistic abilities in order to further develop spoken communication. Crucial to oral success, oralists emphasise, is an educational environment which offers the deaf child plenty of good quality spoken language experience. Many oral educators favour mainstream school settings, especially at the primary stage of education, because there the deaf child is inevitably surrounded by, and obliged to participate in, everyday spoken exchange (Harrison, 1993). Deaf children educated in ordinary schools in Britain can expect to receive regular support from teachers of the deaf. Unit or peripatetic teachers monitor events to ensure that the deaf child's amplification and linguistic needs are being met. Parents, of course, continue to play a crucial role in providing language experience in the home. Special schools with a firm auditory-oral emphasis, where spoken language is the predominant medium of exchange, can also provide the necessary language experience and are in a good position to offer a sensitive language environment and a comprehensive audiological service to support the deaf child's amplification needs. Special schools, where some form of signing is used, inside or out of the classroom, are not generally favoured by oralists. A reliance on signing for communication is believed to detract from the overall auditory-oral experience (Nix, 1981). Wherever he or she is placed it is considered essential by oralists that the deaf child is given every opportunity to develop his listening ability and engage with others in everyday talk.

Learning to read and write, of course, is a major educational goal and oralists believe that for the deaf child, as for children with normal hearing, oracy should form the basis of literacy. When a deaf child can read then the activity of reading itself can further expand vocabulary and reinforce linguistic structures. Deaf children who can read can compensate to an important extent for what they cannot overhear of other people's conversations.

This description of what is entailed in the development of communication and language through an auditory-oral approach does not examine all the many strategies that are available to those using this approach. For the reader who would like a more detailed account, I recommend the following:

Altman, E. (1988) *Talk with me! Giving the Gift of Language and Emotional Health to the Hearing-Impaired Child.* Washington, DC: A.G. Bell Association

Andrews, E. (1988) Conversation. *Journal of the British Association of Teachers of the Deaf* 12, 2, 29–32

Clark, M. (1989) *Language Through Living for Hearing-Impaired Children.* London: Hodder & Stoughton

Harrison, D. (1980) Natural oralism – a description. *Journal of the British Association of Teachers of the Deaf* 4, 4, July Magazine

Lewis, S. and Richards, S. (1988) The early stages of language development: a natural aural approach. *Journal of the British Association of Teachers of the Deaf* 12, 2, 33–38

National Aural Group (1981) Promoting natural language through residual hearing. *Journal of the British Association of Teachers of the Deaf* 5, 3, Magazine Section

Nolan, M. and Tucker, I. (1988) *The Hearing-Impaired Child and the Family*. London: Souvenir Press

Tucker, I. and Powell, C. (1991) *The Hearing Impaired Child and School*. London: Souvenir Press.

What has been described above is what can be broadly termed a 'natural' approach to the development of spoken language in the deaf child because of its heavy emphasis on the use of hearing and on natural language experience. There are variants within the broad category of 'natural oralism' based on different emphases on specific aspects of audition, speech and language. If readers wish to learn about these variations in approach, the following are recommended:

Andrews, E. (1988) The relationship between natural auralism and the maternal reflective way of working. *Journal of the British Association of Teachers of the Deaf* 12, 3, 49–56

Bates, A. (1985) Changes in the approach to encouraging language development in hearing-impaired children. *Journal of the British Association of Teachers of the Deaf* 9, 6, 140–144

Caleffe-Schenck, N. (1990) *Auditory-Verbal Training Program Handbook*. Englewood Co.: The Listen Foundation

Cole, E. (1992) *Listening and Talking: A Guide to Promoting Spoken Language in Young Hearing-Impaired Children*. Washington, DC: A.G. Bell Association

Van Uden, A. (1977) *A World of Language for Deaf Children, Part 1: Basic Principles*. Amsterdam: Swets & Zeitlinger.

The Case for Oralism

The Need for Speech

The ideological basis for the auditory-oral approach to the development of language and communication in deaf children is that verbal communication, in particular spoken communication, is the predominant medium of social exchange. Without the ability to speak and understand the speech of others the individual's links with the wider society are severely restricted, so oralists would argue. It is true that the deaf individual may know sign language and thus have a means of communication but if the deaf individual knows *only* sign language then this will permit communication only with other sign language users, who, generally speaking, will be deaf themselves. However satisfying participation in the Deaf community and in Deaf culture is, it is nonetheless the case that deaf people form a tiny minority within society as a whole*. Deaf people do not live in exclusive deaf neighbour-hoods nor are they employed in exclusive deaf workplaces. Deaf adults are surrounded for most of the time by normally hearing people, and even if the deaf individual chooses most of his or her significant social contact within the Deaf group, the demands of everyday life necessitate a considerable amount of exchange with people who speak and do not sign. If the life opportunities and objectives of the deaf person are to be as wide as those of other people then, so oralists argue, the deaf person needs to be able to interact with reasonable ease and confidence in spoken language.

In theory deaf people who communicate only through sign language can employ the services of hearing sign language interpreters to mediate between themselves and those in the hearing world but, oralists maintain, exchange with others via a third party involves a loss of autonomy and independence. In practice it is most unlikely that the services of sign language interpreters would be available for everyday interaction.

The case for an oral approach in education, say oralists, is not to be viewed as an example of hearing people thinking they 'know what's best' for deaf people and imposing their communication norms and values on the Deaf as a cultural minority. Oralists can refer to the testimony of many orally educated deaf individuals who feel their lives to be considerably expanded through being able to speak, understand speech and partici-pate at a significant level in the hearing world (Ogden, 1982; Lynas, 1986; Briggs, 1991).

For the oralist, then, the goal of speech for deaf people is morally jus-tified on the grounds of individual freedom, independence and ability to participate in the wider society. But is this goal achievable? Can all indi-viduals, deaf from birth, develop fluent spoken communication and an ability to understand the speech of others? A review of the achievements in the past, of deaf children and young people who have received an oral-only education, indicates a notable *lack* of success in bringing spoken language and literacy to the deaf individual (Babbidge, 1965; DES, 1968; Conrad, 1979). These findings from the past seem to suggest that how-ever desirable it might be to enable deaf individuals to talk, the goal is unattainable.

Oralists do not, however, capitulate their case because of poor past achievements. Oralists claim that there are many reasons why oralism 'failed' in the past and that now 'things have changed'. In the first place, hearing aids, the key to the exploitation of residual hearing, were not as effective in the past as they are now nor as widely available. And,

*According to the study of Kyle and Woll (1985) in the county of Avon, England, the deaf population who could be defined as culturally Deaf, represented less than 1:2500 of the total population of the county. The deaf clubs were relatively small: a deaf club with 200 registered members was considered a large one.

secondly, because educators did not have the benefit of insights from modern psycholinguistics, oral educational approaches were often based on erroneous ideas about how language is learned.

Developments in Audiology

To consider first the technological advances in systems of amplification: over the last two decades personal hearing aids available to children have become more powerful over a wider range of speech frequencies (Stone and Adam, 1986). Many deaf children these days are hearing components of speech that 20 or so years ago they would not have been able to hear and this, say oralists, has a crucial bearing on the prospects for the development of speech. Stone and Adam (1986) state:

> Due to technological advances in the past 20 years, it is possible to provide meaningful and important speech information even to most profoundly hearing-impaired children. A child with an unaided auditory response at 500 Hz can be aided so he or she receives the first formant of most vowels, voicing and nasality cues, suprasegmental cues and the transitions of front plosive consonants. Unaided hearing at 1000 Hz can be amplified so the first formants of the mid-vowels, the second formants of the back and mid-vowels, and the second formants of several voiced consonants can be made available. Thus, even children with 'left-corner' or 'ski-slope' audiograms can profit from amplification (p.46).

Hearing aids are also more personalised so that an aid can be adjusted to suit the particular pattern of hearing loss of an individual (Byrne, 1986). The recent development of programmable hearing aids with the advent of digital signal processing applications holds great promise for improved selection and fitting of hearing aids (Staab, 1990). Earmould technology has developed and modern earmoulds are much less likely than in the past to limit the performance of high powered hearing aids (Nolan and Tucker, 1988).

The development of FM systems (radio aids) represents another breakthrough in the development of hearing aids and one that makes a very useful contribution to the deaf child's ability to perceive the spoken word. The main strength of the radio hearing aid is that it enables the wearer to discriminate the speech of another person, such as a teacher or parent, against a background of noise. Radio hearing aids are used by nearly all deaf schoolchildren in the UK and are particularly beneficial in mainstream classrooms which are typically noisy and where acoustic conditions are usually poor (Moodley, 1989). For a good account of the range of radio aids and suggestions for their use, Nolan and Tucker, (1988) is recommended.

A problem with hearing aids in the past, perhaps even more serious than the quality of amplification, has concerned their maintenance. Reports of the day-to-day functioning of hearing aids make dismal reading (Clark, 1989). Martin and Lodge (1969), for example, in the UK, reported that an average of 50% of hearing-impaired children in schools for the deaf and in units for the partially hearing were not making proper use of their hearing aids.

If hearing aids are not carefully managed and maintained, no matter how technologically sophisticated and how good they are when performing optimally, they will not serve the purpose of maximising the deaf child's hearing ability. Whilst it would be over-optimistic to assume that problems no longer exist, oralists believe that there are grounds for thinking that there has been some improvement in the care and supervision of hearing aids in recent years. More teachers of the deaf in the UK take advanced courses in audiology as part of their professional development and most Services for Hearing-Impaired Children will have a member of the team with a specialist qualification in audiology. The development of portable and relatively inexpensive hearing aid test boxes enables more regular and frequent checking of aids. Hearing aid test boxes are easy to use and have become an invaluable support for the checking of aids for peripatetic teachers of the deaf visiting deaf children in their homes and in mainstream schools (Tucker and Powell, 1991).

Availability of hearing aids, of course, is another potentially limiting factor in the management of audition. Fortunately, in the UK, a hearing-impaired child can usually be prescribed any hearing aid that is considered appropriate to his or her needs through the National Health Service. This has not always been the case, however. Up until 1974, children could receive free of charge only hearing aids which were manufactured by the NHS (Kettlety, 1975). NHS hearing aids were not and are not as high-powered as some of the commercial hearing aids. So children with the most substantial hearing losses did not get their amplification needs met unless their parents paid for commercial hearing aids. Hence, the children in the past who had the greatest need for powerful hearing aids probably rarely got them. This factor alone, oralists would claim, could have made all the difference to some deaf children as to whether their audition was being used to develop spoken language.

Another audiological development worth mentioning in relation to the use of residual hearing is the development of audiometric techniques for measuring the hearing of babies. It is possible to measure the hearing of a baby in the first few days of life by physiological testing of the brain's response to sound and there is now considerable experience of fitting hearing aids to tiny babies (Hostler, 1987). Until recently, only babies considered to be 'at risk' were likely to receive this form of audiological assessment. At the present time universal screening by means of physiological tests is taking place or is being considered in many areas of the country. This means that a significantly greater proportion of very deaf children will be identified during the early days or weeks of life and can benefit from amplification during the first year of life. Overall, there is evidence that the age of diagnosis of severe and profound hearing loss continues to fall in the UK (Davis et al., 1988) and this is encouraging to oralists. The sooner the deaf child's hearing is aided the greater the amount of auditory experience in the early years. Research evidence confirms an association between the early fitting of hearing aids in profoundly deaf babies and an increase in vocalisation and speech-like behaviour (Crul, Hoekstra and Suykerbuyk, 1990; Stokes and Bamford, 1990; Robinshaw, 1992).

Finally, a technological advance which affects only a few deaf children in the UK at present, but which may in the future become more significant, is the cochlear implant. A cochlear implant involves inserting a prosthetic device beneath the skull in order to stimulate the auditory nerve neurons. Cochlear implants are designed to convert sounds into electrical energy to stimulate the auditory nerves directly, thereby bypassing the damaged hair cells in the cochlea. Developments in the technology of cochlear implants have resulted in devices which are increasingly capable of providing the individual with the ability to discriminate sounds of different frequencies (Bench, 1992).

Cochlear implants were developed in the first place for adults who had lost their hearing completely or had insufficient hearing to be helped by conventional hearing aids (House, 1976). However, young children with near total hearing losses have more recently been considered suitable candidates for implantation. To assess definite bilateral near total deafness before the age of 2 years is not yet considered possible but the numbers of very deaf children over the age of 2 years who receive cochlear implantation is increasing (Bench, 1992). The reports of improvements in speech perception and speech production are very encouraging to those who are concerned to restore useful hearing to the deafest of the profoundly deaf group (Bouse, 1987; Cunningham, 1990; Geers and Tobey, 1992). Cochlear implants for children are now available in many centres in Western countries, including the UK. The prospect of extending the availability of cochlear implants to all children with very profound hearing losses is welcomed enthusiastically by oralists as a way of reducing the handicap and facilitating communication through audition.

All in all, oralists maintain that the technical and technological advances over the past 20 or so years mean that if we do want to harness the hearing of the deaf child for the development of oral language, then we are in a better position than ever to do so. The ability to provide consistent and high quality listening experience was, in the past, often lacking and this, so oralists would argue, made its contribution to 'oral failure'.

Improved Understanding of Language Development

Our relative lack of understanding of the normal process of language acquisition was another factor, according to the oralist argument, contributing to the poor educational and linguistic achievements of deaf children in the past. However, thanks to the many studies that there have been in recent years on first language acquisition in both normal and abnormal language learners, there has been a significant enlargement of knowledge which is relevant and extremely helpful to those wishing to promote spoken language in deaf children. A major lesson that has been learnt is that language is 'caught' through experience and not "taught" through instruction. Adults are crucial to the language learning process in the early years of childhood not because they teach language but because they offer language experience through interaction (Snow, 1977; Wells, 1981). Rarely do adults 'explain' words or teach grammatical rules to young children: rather they enable language learning to take place out of the dialogue which accompanies normal, everyday activities (Wells, 1986). Now, as already stated, it is not easy for parents to develop conversational exchange with a deaf child. But, given the importance for spoken language development of establishing turn-taking routines and vocal interaction between care-giver and deaf child, most educational Services for Hearing-Impaired Children in the UK devote a significant amount of resources to providing support for parents of young deaf children. Teachers of the deaf, armed with a more refined sensitivity to the process of language acquisition, are now in a better position to offer parents constructive advice which will facilitate the deaf child's spoken language development in the early years.

At school age, educators traditionally have thought that deaf children, because unable easily to assimilate spoken language at normal conversational pace and volume, need deliberate teaching in order to expand their knowledge of the structures of language and the meaning of words. Structured approaches have been used involving explicit teaching of grammar and vocabulary (Bates, 1985). Generally speaking, it is the small and acoustically weak parts of speech which represent 'grammar' – verb inflections, function words, etc. and it is these which are most likely to be elusive to the deaf child. Hence, educators have felt that there was a need to make these grammatical features of language obvious to the deaf child in order to make them accessible. However, concentration on the *form* of language can so easily lead to stilted, artificial, and repetitive language. Observers in special schools for deaf children in the past have attested to the use of stereotyped and oversimplified language (Van Uden, 1977; Ivimey, 1981). Educators in the past, therefore, in their well-intentioned attempt to bring oral language to the deaf child, were offering something that was the very antithesis of living language and real communication. Even children with normal hearing would not be able to acquire their

first language as a consequence of formal teaching and, so modern oralists argue, there is no reason to suppose that deaf children could learn
language in this way. Van Uden (1977), for example, refers to 'constructive methods' as 'the grave of the oral way' with its artificial, teacher-
selected utterances, its 'baked sentences' of the: 'The box is *on* the table'
type. Language that is divorced from communication and natural context, according to oralists, has little or no meaning to a deaf child (Clark,
1989). Current thinking is that deaf children, just like hearing children,
need to make use of all the clues contained in a situation of which spoken
language is a part in order to extract the meaning of communication.
Language itself is learnt almost unconsciously while children are 'learning how to mean' (Tough, 1977). Furthermore, deaf children, just like
hearing children, need experience of the *patterns* of language in order
that their rule-constructing mechanisms can operate. Where adults use
contrived language their speech becomes stilted and the range of grammatical structures reduced. The deaf child is exposed to *less* language not
more than would be offered to a child with the benefit of normal hearing.
Ivimey (1981), for example, having investigated language lessons in classrooms in special schools for the deaf in London, reported that:

> the inescapable conclusion of this is that the practices most frequently
> observed in schools for deaf children are unsuccessful and even counter-
> productive (p.51).

If deaf children do not experience oral language as part of real communication then they are unlikely to use oral language for real communication. Indeed, a further accusation levelled against oral education in
the past is that many educational establishments were not genuinely
'oral' (Clark, 1989). Oral modes of communication were at best to be
found only inside the classsroom. Outside the classroom deaf children
would typically communicate through sign (Kretschmer and
Kretschmer, 1978). Clark (1989) suggests that, since the 'oral' approach
offered was so 'rigid and restricted', it is little wonder that the deaf
pupils 'are more at home expressing themselves in sign'. In such circumstances the development of fluent spoken communication is
believed to be doomed to failure.

A policy of using structured language approaches in schools is not the
only reason, according to oralists, for flawed practice in the name of oralism. As stated earlier, when adults address deaf children it is difficult to
sustain conversational interaction. The relative lack of responsiveness of
deaf children can have a severe inhibiting effect on the speech of the
teacher and 'unnatural' and often very restricted language can result.
(For some illuminating examples of the problems teachers can have
when addressing groups of deaf children, see Wood et al., 1986).
However, given that we now have insight into the potential difficulties of

establishing conversational exchange with deaf children oralists claim that we can take steps to overcome the problems. For example, responding contingently to what a child might be thinking or feeling, listening and watching for the child's communicative overtures, pausing to allow the child to contribute to the exchange — all these strategies can significantly increase the locquacity of the deaf child and improve the flow of conversation (Wood et al., 1986). Knowing what was going wrong, say oralists, enables us to 'get it right'.

Modern oralists agree, then, that an overemphasis on language itself, rather than on communication *through* language, leads to a restriction rather than an enlargement of the deaf child's language experience: verbal language will not be internalised unless it is used for real communication. Succumbing to the impact of deafness on communication can, similarly, impose a severe restriction on language input and on conversational exchange.

Given the conviction of oralists concerning the importance of natural language for linguistic progress, many oral educators believe that the trend towards educating increasing numbers of children with severe and profound hearing losses in ordinary schools has contributed to greater success with the oral approach (Lynas, 1986; Harrison, 1993). In the ordinary school environment the majority of children and adults are using verbal language in a natural way, and in a range of contexts, and deaf children can benefit from a rich experience of spoken language used by competent speakers. What better place to 'catch' language than where spoken language is the predominant medium of exchange, so many oralists argue (Harrison, 1993). Deaf children in the mainstream school are challenged not only to speak intelligibly but also to make best use of their residual hearing in order to communicate with others. Many studies indicate that spoken language ability increases with the oralness of the environment (Quigley and Kretschmer, 1982; Paul and Quigley, 1990). However, most oralists agree that good spoken language experience can also be provided in a special school. Given that the deaf child is provided with the best possible amplification and with the kind of language experience which promotes language acquisition and development, the actual location of education is unimportant. Support for oral special schools continues and oral educators within them claim to be aware of the 'traps' associated with a special school environment and to be able to offer a 'rich language enabling environment' (Clark, 1989).

Whilst oralists stress the goal of spoken language, the aim of literacy is also strongly emphasised. Here, oralists join the advocates of other approaches in believing that the ability to read is essential for access to socially shared knowledge and for the full development of intellectual potential. What oralists argue, however, is that the only *known* route to literacy is through oral language. Unimpaired language learners base their literacy on their spoken language, the primary form of verbal language, (Beard, 1990) and, so the argument goes, this has to be the 'way into' literacy for deaf children. Written language is just another form of verbal language and the two are closely related. The written form of English and other European languages is phonologically based: that is, there is a relationship between the written symbols and the spoken symbols. The task of learning to read, therefore, is one of encoding from one form of verbal language to another. There is much evidence that children, generally, who have poor oracy have poor literacy (Clark, 1976). This, according to oralists, supports the belief that oracy, or at least an internal representation of spoken language, is a necessary condition for access to verbal language in the written form (Quigley and Paul, 1984).

Some recent research by Schaper and Reitsma (1993), in Holland, investigated the extent to which deaf chidren used speech-based codes in reading processes. The study examined the coding strategies for reading of 78 pre-lingually, orally educated children aged 6–13 years. The results revealed a developmental change in the use of coding strategies: up to 9 years most of the children seemed to process written words by means of visual codes. Beyond the age of 9 years almost all the children employed a speech-based code to some extent, although some appeared to continue to use predominantly visual strategies. Those children who used predominantly a speech-based code were, however, better in reading performance. The investigation supports the idea that promoting the acquisition of spoken language will promote the development of literacy.

The present position of oralists, then, is that largely as a result of advances in technology, an enlargement of knowledge of the way language works and improved educational practice, things have never been better for the achievement of the goal of spoken language in even the deafest of children (National Aural Group, 1981). And, oralists emphasise, the goal *is* realistic: although careful management is of vital importance, and the provision of conditions which are propitious to the development of spoken language is by no means easy, it does not require out of the ordinary ability nor superhuman effort. Providing the specialist services and equipment which support an auditory-oral approach does involve financial expense and human expertise but, so oralists would argue, the resource requirements are likely to be no greater (and probably much less) than those entailed with other communication options.

Evidence Supporting an Auditory-Oral Approach

Having presented the reasoning oralists might use to support the case for an auditory-oral approach it is clearly essential to look at recent research findings on the achievements of orally educated children. The 'proof of the pudding is in the eating' and if what oralists say is true, then recent evidence should confirm that deaf young people, educated by an oral approach, are achieving fluent and intelligible oral communication and a mastery of verbal language including the written form. The problem for oralists in much of the writing advocating an auditory-oral approach, e.g. Nolan and Tucker, (1988); Clark, (1989), is the lack of 'hard evidence' about the actual achievements of orally educated deaf children. There is evidence, however, from three recent investigations: one from the USA and two from the UK and these will now be considered.

The US study by Geers and Moog (1989) involved 100 hearing-impaired young people aged 16 and 17 years from the USA and Canada: they were enrolled on oral programmes, and most (85%) were mainstreamed for all or most of the day. All the subjects had a hearing loss greater than 85 dB HL: half had better ear unaided thresholds 85–100 dB HL and the other half had hearing losses greater than 100 dB HL. All had a performance IQ above 85 and the average was 111.

The authors give good background and demographic data — better than is usual with studies on the achievements of deaf children (Bench, 1992). The socio-economic status of the families of the subjects was generally above average. On the whole the parents were highly supportive — with 90% or more reporting that they helped their children in a variety of ways and on a regular basis with speech, language and academic work. Ninety per cent of the children had been fitted with hearing aids by age 2 years and 54% by age 1 year. The average age first aided was 21 months. Seventy-five per cent had been enrolled in some form of parent–infant programme by age 2 years and 63% had been enrolled in pre-school special education by age 3 years.

Geers and Moog (1989) point out that whilst the socio-economic and early intervention data might indicate a highly select group, the sample represents around half of the orally educated profoundly deaf 16–17 year olds in North America. (Nearly 90% of profoundly deaf children in North America, 1985-1986, were in TC programmes, (Schildroth and Hotto, 1991).) So, the sample is representative of the orally educated children in North America.

The subjects were tested for abilities in reading, writing, spoken and sign language, speech perception and production and cognition. The findings were as follows:

Mean grade level for reading comprehension was 8th grade which is equivalent to 13–14 years

Thirty per cent had reading skills at or above 10th grade which is equivalent to 16 years

Only 15% had reading ability less than 3rd grade, that is around 8 years or less

The majority were able to write an acceptable essay and business letter with only some grammatical and mechanical errors

Sixty per cent demonstrated word recognition skills through listening alone

Eighty-eight per cent demonstrated proficiency with spoken English from both a language and speech intelligibility point of view

Verbal intelligence scores were in the average range when compared with normally hearing adolescents

Only 9% demonstrated any sign language proficiency.

The authors conclude:

> The sample of hearing-impaired subjects in this study exhibited abilities in many areas that were above-average for hearing-impaired adolescents in general (p. 83).

Geers and Moog (1989) refer to the data reported on the achievements of profoundly deaf children in America overall which indicate that the average reading age of 16–17-year-olds is below 3rd grade level, that is: 8 years or below (Allen, 1986).

Oralists judge these results to be impressive and supportive of their claim. Most of the young people, despite profound hearing impairment, had achieved literacy as well as fluent and intelligible spoken communication. With continuing education there is no reason to suppose that the linguistic attainments would not continue to rise.

The authors acknowledge a combination of favourable factors: at least average non-verbal intellectual ability; reasonably early diagnosis; early educational intervention and auditory stimulation; predominantly middle class families; strong family support. But oralists would claim that many of the favourable conditions associated with these features could apply to all profoundly deaf children if policy makers so wished. So, for example, if it were felt that there was insufficient parental support steps could be taken to help the family, or some members of it, to be more supportive in providing appropriate language experience and in taking good care of hearing aids. A more concerted effort to detect hearing loss in the early months could lead to the earlier diagnosis of profound deafness in children.

The first UK study to be considered is that of Harrison, Simpson and Stuart (1991). This research involved 86 non-selected pre-lingually deaf children living in Leicestershire, England, representing a range of social classes and ethnic groups. The age range was 5–17 years. All the children had been educated through an auditory-oral and interactive approach to the acquisition of language and communication. Samples of the children's free written language were analysed and put into one of five categories according to their syntactic maturity or completeness. There were 28 children who had hearing losses greater than 90 dB and we shall consider only the results relating to these children.

Category Two written language was achieved by seven of the children. Category Two language was described as 'Generally accurate use of syntax with only occasional errors involving the use of tenses, word endings or the omission of functors. The majority of the sentences are wholly correct'. An example of Category Two writing:

M.S., Chronological age 11;10 years, Av. hearing loss better ear 103 dB.

Do you remember me talking about the gerbils? Well Jennifer the mother had died on Jan 2nd and I was very upset. The other are fine. Me, Ian my brother and dad had been taking Whisky the cat to the vet because we didn't know what was wrong with Whisky foot. Dad was driving with Ian in the front seat and I was left in the back with whisky and is was really funny because he went all over the place. At home after the visit to the vet dad told me what the vet said, he said that Whisky had been bitten by a cat and he got two holes in his paw.

Category Three written language was achieved by 15 children. Category Three language was described as 'Fluent and expressive use of complex language allowing easy extraction of meaning, though with clearly immature syntax evidenced by frequent errors involving endings, the omission of functors and the incorrect use of tenses'. An example of Category Three writing:

R.M., Chronological age 11;5 years, Av. hearing loss better ear 114 dB.

A little boy at christmas.

One day it was christmas. There a little boy he was very excited and shouted 'IT CHRISTMAS DAY AND SANTA IS COMING TONIGHT'. And his mummy said 'Calm down'. He went upstair and his mum said to him 'Leon where are you going?' 'I'm going to bed because I might couldn't go to sleep'. Then his parent went to bed too, and Santa came to Leon house but Leon did not go to sleep because he was just pretending because he want to see a santa but he didn't get out of the bed because he too frightened because if he get out of the bed and the santa might tell his parent.

Category Four writing was achieved by two of the profoundly deaf children. Category Four writing was described as 'Characterised by the use of simple sentences with correct word order, with little use of functors, word endings often omitted and little variety in the use of tenses'. An example of Category Four writing:

C.D., Chronological age 9;4 years. Av. hearing loss better ear 116 dB.

Fall over bike. Big stone. Fall over bike. Cry Mummy help. Face scratch. Arm scratch. Hand scratch two legs, scratch. very very bleed.

Category Five writing was achieved by four of the children. Category Five writing is described as 'Emergent writing. Two or three word sentences or phrases. No word endings, tenses not differentiated, only occasional use of functors. Extracting meaning likely to require knowledge of the context'. An example of Category Five writing:

S.M. Chronological Age 8;4 years, Average hearing loss, better ear 128 dB.

The window happy
winter lovely
The snowball girl boy
The bang cold brrr shiver
The postman tomorrow is ByeBye snowman
The cold Ha-Ha-Ha hat glove The End

This rather full reporting of the writing of these profoundly deaf children from Leicestershire aims to indicate that overall much higher standards of writing were achieved than are normally found within this category of hearing loss. According to Quigley and Kretschmer (1982):

It is probably fair to say that most deaf students do not attain even adequate ability to read and write English (p. 66).

Yet, 22 out of the 28 profoundly deaf children who featured in the investigation were clearly achieving 'adequate' levels of writing in terms of fluency, accuracy and syntactical complexity. It can be safely concluded, given that the writing was spontaneous and uncorrected, that these written attainments reflected a satisfactory command of the structures of English: an internal representation of oral language*. The remaining six were achieving standards similar to those reported for deaf children generally (Arnold, 1978), that is, with 'deviant structures'. However, it should be noted that none of the children achieving Category Four writing were above the age of 10;7 years, and none of the children in Category Five were above the age of 11;5 years. It would not be unfair to assume that some of these children were displaying immaturity rather then deviance in their writing and that it would, in time, improve.

The Leicestershire research, oralists claim, supports the assertion that with good use of residual hearing and a natural aural approach, deaf children can acquire language (Harrison, Simpson and Stuart, 1991).

The other UK study to be considered was undertaken by Lewis (1994). As part of the study Lewis investigated the reading levels of 82 young people of school leaving age, 15–17 years, with hearing losses greater than 65 dB HL. The pupils selected had received a minimum of five years'

---

*A subsequent analysis of the reading abilities of the deaf children in Leicestershire confirms the 'good' standards of literacy indicated by the written language study (Simpson, Harrison and Stuart, 1992).

education within natural oral programmes: they were drawn from two special schools, and four LEA Services, all of which had a well established tradition of using a natural oral approach. The reading measures used were the same as those employed by Conrad (1979) in his study of deaf school leavers in order that the results could be compared. The mean IQ (non-verbal) of the group was 103 and the median IQ was 105.

The reading levels achieved by the young people featuring in the Lewis study were as follows:

Mean Reading Age: 12;10

Median Reading Age: 13;4.

There was no relationship between level of hearing loss and reading age as the following data indicate:

Table 2.1 Levels of hearing loss and reading age

Hearing loss (dB HL)	Number of pupils	Median reading age (years)
66–85	17	13
86–95	16	13;7
96–105	24	12;10
106+	25	13;8

Seventy-six per cent had reading ages of 11 years or above; 14.6% had reading ages less than 9 years and 4.88% failed to score on the test. There was a significant but small relationship between reading age and non-verbal IQ.

The literacy achievements investigated by Lewis are not dissimilar to those reported by Geers and Moog (1989) despite the fact that the average non-verbal IQ of the group was lower than that of the Geers and Moog sample. The Lewis group was, however, similar in terms of IQ to Conrad's (1979) school leavers, yet the reading levels are considerably higher — the overall median was nearly 13 years compared to below 9 years for the Conrad group. Overall, Lewis's young people were 'deafer' than the Conrad sample, with 79% having a hearing loss of 85 dB HL or more compared with 59% with a hearing loss of 85 dB HL or more in Conrad's population. In the Conrad study, 50% of those with hearing losses greater than 85 dB HL failed to score on the reading test whilst only 4.88% (all profoundly deaf) of the Lewis sample failed to achieve a reading score. Within each hearing loss band the Lewis sample was superior to the Conrad sample and the differences became more marked with higher levels of hearing loss: in the Conrad study there was a significant relationship between hearing level and reading level, but with the Lewis sample there was no such relationship.

That 14.6% of Lewis's young people had reading levels less than 9 years is judged by the author to indicate that 'clearly there is still room for improvement'. However, with the Lewis sample it is the *majority* who are achieving good standards of functional literacy rather than the minority which was the case in the Conrad study. This is, of course, pleasing to oralists and supportive of their conviction that the modern auditory-oral approach is a genuine improvement on the 'oralism' of 20 or so years ago.

Problems with Oralism

Language Delay

Oralists acknowledge that with an auditory-oral approach profoundly deaf children typically do not learn to listen immediately they are fitted with hearing aids and that spoken language acquisition takes longer than when a child has normal hearing or a less severe hearing loss (Nolan and Tucker, 1988; Clark, 1989). This delay does not seem to prevent profoundly deaf children eventually mastering the structures of verbal language and this confirms research elsewhere that if there is a 'critical period' for language learning this period is not the first five years of life (Mogford and Bishop, 1988). However, delay in language acquisition does mean that some deaf children cannot communicate through language during the early years in quite the same way as a hearing child. The frustration caused by this delay has led some to believe that deaf children suffer serious emotional problems which may persist into adulthood (Meadow, 1980). Oralists respond to this accusation by claiming that there is no evidence, other than conjecture, of *permanent* emotional disturbance or psychological damage in orally educated children or adults. Furthermore, there *is* evidence which indicates that deaf adults with good verbal ability show no personality differences from the normative patterns of normally hearing young adults (Levine, 1976).

However, there may be a problem when the language-delayed deaf child starts school. Most profoundly deaf children in the UK start school in the mainstream where there is the general assumption that the structures of language of the new pupils are 'in place': that is, by the age of five it is assumed that children have already acquired all the grammar of their first language and a wide vocabulary of everyday words. The deaf child, with linguistic structures still to acquire and a relatively small vocabulary, can be seen to be at a disadvantage because linguistically less well equipped to receive the education that is offered. The oralist response is that with appropriate support in the ordinary infant school an educationally profitable time is possible. Many of the activities in the infant classroom do not demand high levels of linguistic competence and it is not at the infant stage that teachers offer a lot of factual information. Early reading-books generally use simple linguistic structures and basic vocabulary.

That so many profoundly deaf children in the UK are receiving their education in the context of the mainstream infant school suggests that their supporting teachers of the deaf probably believe that the placement is suitable and the educational experience worthwhile. It is not unreasonable, so oralists argue, to suppose that the social and learning environment of the infant classroom, with its many opportunities for talk on a variety of topics, may help accelerate the language development of the deaf child.

The Struggle to Communicate and Acquire Knowledge

Even if we agree that a rich oral environment, whether offered by a mainstream school or by a special oral school for the deaf, provides a facilitating context for the acquisition of spoken language and literacy, and even if the deaf pupil has acquired a good command of verbal language, it can be argued that to receive an education exclusively by the oral medium means a constant, difficult struggle for the deaf child. The deaf child is always at a disadvantage relative to hearing children in receiving information via the spoken word: the deaf child must concentrate harder with both eyes and ears to keep abreast of lesson material (Lynas, 1986). Furthermore, to be obliged to communicate throughout the day through spoken language increases the burden. This is particularly so for the mainstreamed deaf child who is surrounded by competent hearer-speakers and who is likely to be reminded frequently of his hearing handicap by failures to grasp what is being said and by an inability to participate fully in the cut-and-thrust of informal school life. Mainstreaming is particularly singled out by critics of oralism for imposing an unacceptable strain on the deaf pupil. The accounts of some deaf individuals who have been educated in ordinary schools and colleges suggest that to be educated entirely through a communication approach designed for those with normal hearing can be stressful and undermining (Lawson, 1981; Ladd, 1981; Reid, 1991).

The oralists respond to this criticism by acknowledging that it is undoubtedly difficult to be deaf in a hearing society but that an oral education offers the best preparation for participation in the hearing world. Acquiring an education through oral means is not easy but, so far, the oral approach seems to offer the widest educational opportunity in terms of academic achievements. It is, furthermore, not the case that *all* deaf children and young people feel negative about their oral education. The present author investigated the attitudes of orally educated children and young people, many of whom were profoundly deaf, all of whom had educational experience in mainstream schools (Lynas, 1986). The research indicated positive views towards both oral education and mainstreaming. Difficulties were reported, but, on the whole, the subjects appreciated the challenge and believed that an oral education in the ordinary school offered them both good education and the 'best preparation for life'. Recent testimony from a profoundly deaf young person, reporting on her success in Higher Education, confirms that there is support from deaf people for an oral education:

> Indeed, it is true that if I had not been educated orally, I would not be where I am now. This is sad but a fact of life which perhaps British Sign Language supporters do not recognise. ... We must be realistic as deaf people do form a minority in society and thus we cannot expect all hearing people to learn Sign Language for the benefit of a few deaf people whom they may never encounter anyway (Briggs, 1991, p. 109).

Suppression of Deaf Identity

An issue considered particularly serious by many critics of oralism is that the premises underlying an oral education, in particular an oral education in the mainstream, are morally wrong. An oral education, it is alleged, implies that the deaf child should assimilate into the hearing world and become 'normalised'. The deaf child is required to conform as far as possible to the norms of hearing society. That this is a violation of justice as well as cruel is expressed graphically by Treesburg (1990) who likens oralism to the tradition of footbinding in China:

> At the speech and hearing clinic, I was trained to bind the mind of my daughter. Like the twisting of feet into lotus hooks, I was encouraged to force her deaf mind into a hearing shape (p. 1).

A deaf child, so it is argued, can never become more than a 'pale imitation' of a hearing person (Ladd, 1981). Moreover, encouraging the deaf child to take on the social identity of a hearing person is to deny the child access to his 'true' identity, which is that of a Deaf person. An oral education in the mainstream, according to this view, denies deafness and implies an attempt to make a deaf child be what he or she can never be: a hearing person (Merrill, 1981).

Oralists respond to this criticism by agreeing that deafness *does* impose certain limitations in a hearing society. Oralists also acknowledge that encouraging deaf children to associate with hearing children and adults is likely to foster identification with those who can hear but they do not agree that this is a bad thing: to become accustomed to being deaf in a hearing world from an early age is believed by oralists to be beneficial. Furthermore, with appropriate support and understanding deaf children and young people need not feel undermined or unconfident in the world of hearing-speaking people (Dale, 1984;

Lynas 1986; Bishop, Gregory and Sheldon, 1991). Oralists, supportive of mainstream education for deaf children, reject the accusation that an ordinary school education implies a 'denial' of deafness and that it forces on the deaf unnatural social experience. On the contrary, an education in the mainstream, so the oralist argument goes, allows the mutual acceptance of deaf and hearing individuals and a shared respect for differences. Both deaf and hearing children have the opportunity to learn that we are all different in some respects and that we all have weaknesses and strengths. Furthermore, whilst growing up in the midst of hearing people does not, it is true, promote a sense of belonging to the Deaf community or of having a special 'Deaf' identity, there are plenty of opportunities for the deaf individual to become part of the 'Deaf world' as they grow up if they want to do so. Who is stopping the deaf child or young person from joining the local deaf club if he so wishes? It seems unlikely that even the most devout of oralists would wish to interfere with any deaf child's choice of social activity outside school.

Persistence of Oral 'Failure'

A difficulty for oralists, and a matter on which they are not all agreed, is whether or not *all* deaf children, in particular those with very little residual hearing, can achieve acceptable levels of communicative competence through an auditory-oral approach. Are there a minority of profoundly deaf children who, no matter how 'perfect' the amplification and language experience, cannot achieve mastery of verbal language nor intelligible speech through audition? It is the case that, for whatever reason, some deaf children who have had a 'pure' auditory-oral environment do not develop fluent oral communication nor command of the structures and vocabulary of verbal language. For example, there were a minority of the sample involved in the Geers and Moog (1989) study, cited above, who did not achieve proficiency in spoken language and did not achieve literacy. In the sample featuring in the Lewis study, 14.6% had reading ages which were less than 9 years.

Some writers think that there are differences in children's psycho-perceptual abilities and that when a child is very deaf this feature can have a crucial influence on the ability of some children to make use of residual hearing (Bamford and Saunders, 1991). Tumim (1982), for example, on the basis of her experience with her two deaf daughters (one of whom developed oral language relatively easily whilst the other did not) believes that the ability to perceive the prosodic features of speech is a crucial factor. The daughter who acquired spoken language relatively easily was, in audiometric terms, deafer than her sister but could perceive the intonation patterns of speech, whereas her sister could not.

If there are 'within-child' features which, regardless of the auditory and linguistic environment, will limit the development of oral communicative competence then it would be useful to be able to diagnose these features at an early stage in the child's life in order to allow alternative communication options to be used effectively. However, it does not seem as if any such diagnostic technique exists. Attempts have been made to develop a set of indicators of oral competence (Geers and Moog, 1987) but there seems to be a problem of confounding the indices which predict with the outcomes of experience. So, for example, the Spoken Language Predictor devised by Geers and Moog puts 'language competence' and 'speech communication attitudes' as major predictors of later spoken language competence. But, it could be that language competence and speech attitudes are themselves the result of good early auditory and spoken language experience. That a child does not at the time of assessment have the 'requisite' features does not necessarily mean that he or she does not have the potential to develop spoken language.

Geers and Moog (1987) also suggest that innate intellectual ability influences the abilility of the profoundly deaf child to succeed orally. However, although above average intelligence has been found to support oral competence, the Lewis (1994) evidence cited above suggests that IQ *per se* is a significant but not a very 'weighty' factor. So, good intellectual ability may be a helpful feature but, so oralists believe, not a necessary condition for oral success.

Oralists tend to prefer to think that it is experience which is all important rather than actual or imputed psychological or psycho-perceptual features: oral 'failure' has considerably reduced over the last 10–15 years and oralists believe that some of the current 'failure' is a consequence not of the auditory-oral approach per se but of poor implementation of that approach. Most oralists would argue, anyway, that *all* children, however deaf, should be *given the chance* to develop oral language through a natural auditory approach since we do not know in the early stages how well a child can hear or perceive speech. It may be the case that some deaf children need relatively more spoken language experience to 'break the barrier', but if we do not offer an auditory-oral approach we may lose forever the chance to enable the child to learn to listen and perceive speech. Developments in cochlear implantation, described above, offer fresh support to oralists for the idea that *all* deaf children can be enabled to hear and discriminate speech.

Many educators, who would call themselves oralists, nonetheless believe that there are some deaf children who, for a variety of reasons, cannot or do not make acceptable oral progress. For these children there is the view that an alternative, probably 'easier' communication option, such as some form of signing, is appropriate. On the issue of *when* to take the decision that oralism is 'failing' a deaf child there is, however, no agreement. There are varying notions about how long it is reasonable to wait for audition and speech to become established. Also, when signing is seen as a solution only for those who do not make oral progress, it is only too easy to perceive the signing option as a relegation and the child himself as the 'failure'. This can be seen as an unacceptable indictment of sign language and indeed of the deaf child, but the alternative of abandoning oralism at the outset is even more unacceptable because it denies the opportunity to speak to those who could do so. There are, however, no easy solutions to the problem of 'oral failure' and, given the existence and recognition of sign as a means of communication, it is becoming increasingly unacceptable for educators to persist with a pure oral approach throughout the school years, if a child shows little evidence of understanding the spoken word.

The Need for Perfect Conditions

There is a view which accepts that fluent spoken language is a desirable goal and that many deaf children have the potential to achieve it but that in practice the goal is only achievable under certain conditions. These conditions, it is argued, are often too difficult to meet. McAnally, Rose and Quigley (1987), referring to practices and provision in the USA state:

> oral-aural approaches are difficult to use and seem to require special conditions for success, conditions that cannot easily be met in the public school system (p. 202).

According to this view the demands of the auditory-oral approach, with the necessity for consistently good hearing aid maintenance and management and the need for a facilitating oral language environment both at home and at school, are beyond the capacity of many, if not most, parents and educators. However, in Britain, the idea that oralism only works if there is a combination of favourable factors has been challenged (Tucker, 1986; Clark, 1989).

Tucker (1986), for example, reports good oral progress in a sample of pre-school children, most of whom came from low socio-economic families. He believes, with many other oralist educators, that most families, if given sufficient support and guidance, *can* provide an appropriate oral language environment at home. Furthermore, whilst communicating with a very deaf pre-school child is not easy for anyone, it is surely easier, Tucker says, for hearing parents of any social category, to communicate through their own language than to attempt to do so with a new medium such as sign language*. Also, children and adults in the local community

*It is estimated that only 3% of severely or profoundly deaf children (that is, children with average hearing losses greater than 70 dB) have both parents who are deaf and a further 7% have one parent who is deaf.

are important potential providers of language experience for the deaf child and they, of course, will be fluent in spoken language. So oralists subscribe to the view of Ivimey (1981) that:

> only by making use of the existing skills of each child's parents and their friends and acquaintances, and so on can we ensure that the child will be in a position to enjoy a wide experience of language. Without this, he is unlikely to be able to construct the necessary internal linguistic models (p. 58).

Clark (1989) claims there have been good oral achievements for many deaf children and young people despite a combination of *un*favourable factors, for example, low socio-economic category families, late diagnosis, badly fitting earmoulds and inconsistent use of hearing aids in the early years. This is not to say that the presence or otherwise of these features and circumstances have no significance but that they are not, as it is claimed, *crucial* factors. The potentially adverse effects can, with appropriate educational and audiological services, be redressed.

That schools cannot routinely create the conditions supportive of the development of spoken language can also be challenged. There is no logical reason why teachers using an auditory-oral approach need to be 'superpersons' any more than with any other communication approach. Teachers working with deaf children do need to be sensitive to language use, in particular their own, and they do need to be aware of how language is acquired. However, an understanding of how language 'works' is important for all educators of deaf children regardless of communication method.

Audiological knowledge sufficient to monitor the behaviour of hearing aids so that the deaf child gets maximum benefit from them is a necessary requirement for oral teachers working in most contexts. Almost all teachers of the deaf in the UK serve children with a wide range of hearing losses. Most of these children have hearing losses which are less than profound and they wear hearing aids. Few would dispute the benefit these children derive from the hearing aids. Teachers of the deaf, therefore, are accustomed to working with hearing aid users and generally perceive it as part of their job to ensure that their hearing aids are well maintained and managed. Hence, UK teachers of the deaf do not have to learn new skills when dealing with the amplification needs of profoundly deaf children; they are simply applying what they already know. And besides, for TC and bilingualism a fluency in sign is required. It could certainly be argued that acquiring competence in a sign system or sign language requires at least as much, if not more, effort and ability as acquiring appropriate audiological knowledge.

Providing hearing aids and ensuring that they are well maintained is costly but is not likely to be any more expensive than providing specialised training in, say, Signed English or British Sign Language. In any case, if a major criticism of oralism is that it is unattainable because of inadequate resources then there are ethical problems with that position. If a 'desirable' oral education can be offered to only a minority of deaf children then there is clearly a problem of injustice, especially if that minority are primarily deaf children of relatively wealthy, middle class parents. This lack of equality of opportunity based on socio-economic category may be more of a North American problem than a UK one where, traditionally in the USA, hearing aids have to be paid for privately and some of the established oral programmes are private and fee paying. With poverty and privatisation on the increase in the UK it is perhaps worth being forewarned about the possibility of deaf children from economically impoverished homes not having an equal chance of what might be considered to be the best education. It is doubtful if supporters of alternative communication options would welcome being perceived as legitimising 'education on the cheap'.

So, in response to the view that the auditory-oral approach is desirable but too demanding, oralists say that the oral approach, because desirable, should be accessible to all deaf children. Discrimination on financial grounds is unacceptable. Providing optimum amplification consistently and offering enriching language experience to all profoundly deaf children is not *easily* achieved but it is, say oralists, achievable. Oralists could claim that in comparison with what is entailed with TC or bilingualism, oralism is probably the easiest approach to apply.

Chapter 3
Total Communication

Total Communication (TC) involves the use of sign as well as speech in order to develop the language and communication of deaf children. TC originated in the USA and became very popular there during the 1970s. According to the 'Annual Survey of Hearing Impaired Children and Youth' conducted 1989–90 by the Gallaudet University Research Institute, 88% of profoundly deaf children were being educated with the use of signs as well as speech (Schildroth and Hotto, 1991). We do not have precise figures of TC use in the UK but there is evidence that the use of sign in a TC approach has increased, in particular over the last decade, both in special schools and units (Jordan, 1982; Mitchell, 1984; Powers, 1990; Child, 1991; Bloor, 1993).

What is Involved in a Total Communication Approach?

TC involves the use of *all* modalities of communication – sign, finger spelling, speech, hearing, lipreading, facial expression and gesture. By having access to all channels of communication, it is believed that the deaf child can make use of all his or her sensory mechanisms to develop language and acquire a means of communication. The most important aspect of TC is the acceptance of the principle of using whatever means of communication promotes effective communication and linguistic understanding. Generally speaking, this means making use of signs in order to clarify meaning. By making greater use of the visual medium, and the deaf child's unimpaired sense of vision, there is an emphasis on what the child *can* do. TC has been described as:

> a philosophy incorporating appropriate aural, manual and oral modes of communication in order to ensure effective communication with and among hearing-impaired persons (Garretson, 1976, p. 91).

The TC approach aims to get 'the best of all worlds' from a communication point of view. The most common embodiment of TC is the use of speech simultaneously with a signed version of all or part of the spoken utterance. The signs which accompany the speech represent the words of the utterance and are, therefore, a manual–visual form of that speech. Denton (1976), from the USA, recognised as one of the 'founding fathers' of TC, summarises his concept of TC:

> In regard to the day to day practical aspects of Total Communication, the concept simply means that, in so far as possible, those persons within the child's immediate environment should talk and sign simultaneously, and the child should be benefiting from appropriate amplification. ... The highly visual and dramatic language of signs operate as the foundation of Total Communication reinforcing, undergirding and clarifying those minimal clues available through speechreading. Likewise, minimal auditory clues are enhanced and reinforced by signs and speechreading (p. 6).

The signing used in simultaneous communication (sim-com) is not the same as the signing used by members of the Deaf community. Natural sign languages, such as American Sign Language (ASL) and British Sign Language (BSL), which have evolved over the years through use by deaf people, have a structure which is very different from the structure of English. BSL is not a manual–visual form of English and is not, therefore, suitable for use simultaneously with speech. The signing used in a TC or sim-com approach in Britain is a contrived system of signs, based on the signs of BSL, but presented in English word order. It is only in this way, so it is believed, that signs can reinforce the spoken words. There are two main variants of sign used in sim-com in Britain, Signed English and Sign Supported English. Both systems make use of finger spelling.

Signed English

Signed English (SE) is designed to represent English with full respect to the grammar of English. Hence, not only are signs presented in English word order, but are extended to include English syntactical features. There are invented signs to represent verb inflections, adverbial and adjectival endings, plurality, possession, etc. and invented signs to represent the function words, such as *a, the, as, of, at*, etc. So, whilst the 'content' signs are borrowed from BSL or ASL, the reformulation of them for SE makes BSL or ASL and SE very different from each other. In SE, finger spelling is used to supplement signs: that is, where there is no sign corresponding to a word in English, each individual letter of the word is spelt out on the fingers.

The essential feature of SE is that *every* element of the spoken message is represented visually because the aim is to bring verbal language in all its complexity to the deaf child. In SE the intention is to deliver the spoken and signed messages synchronously. It is expected that the deaf child will receive the signs of SE and associated lip patterns of speech through vision and the sounds of spoken English using the best available amplification system. The full presentation of English in an audio-visual form is believed to provide the child with a substantial hearing impairment the best possible chance of receiving and developing language.

Sign Supported English

Sign Supported English (SSE) differs from SE in that there is no attempt to present every element of the spoken utterance. With SSE, it is not necessary to sign or finger spell every word in the spoken utterance. Generally speaking it is the function words, inflections and other markers which are omitted. As with SE the intention is to synchronise the signs with the corresponding spoken element. The purpose of SSE is to clarify the spoken message, lessen ambiguity and emphasise new or key words rather than provide a complete manual–visual language.

Finger Spelling

Finger spelling means literally spelling on the fingers the alphabet of a language. In English there are 26 hand positions corresponding to the 26 letters of the alphabet which can be used to spell out a word. In the UK the manual alphabet is two-handed; in the USA and in most other countries a one-handed system is used. Finger spelling is a useful component of manual–visual forms of English, in particular for introducing names, new or technical terms. Finger spelling is a rather slow form of communication, so it is recommended that it should not be over-used as a component of SE.

With a TC approach, making use of the child's residual hearing is considered essential and, therefore, there should be the same careful attention to amplification and hearing aids as there is with an auditory-oral approach. In addition, however, once deafness is diagnosed in a child, parents and perhaps other relatives and close friends of the family should learn to sign. The advantage of SE or SSE is that the signing follows the pattern of English and is, therefore, claimed to be relatively easy to learn. There are many sign language classes available in most areas of Britain so that parents should not have too much difficulty in obtaining lessons. It is also important that teachers of deaf children become competent at signing as it is considered essential that TC is an available strategy for communication throughout the school years.

For more detailed descriptions of what is entailed with a TC approach, I recommend the following:

Bench, R.J. (1992) *Communication Skills in Hearing-Impaired Children*, London: Whurr, Ch. 5

Bornstein, H. (1974) *Signed English: a manual approach to English language development.* Journal of Speech and Hearing Disorders 39, 330–343

Bornstein, H. (Ed.) (1990) *Manual Communication: Implications for Education*, Washington, DC: Gallaudet University Press

Evans, L. (1982) *Total Communication: Structure and Strategy.* Washington, DC: Gallaudet University Press

Freeman, R.D., Carbin, C.F. and Boese, R.J. (1981) *Can't Your Child Hear? A Guide for Those who Care about Deaf Children.* Baltimore: University Park Press.

The Case for a TC Approach

It is not difficult to understand the appeal of using a TC approach, particularly in the light of the surveys in the 1960s and 1970s of the achievements of orally educated deaf children, (Myklebust, 1964; Babbidge, 1965; DES, 1968; Conrad, 1979; Ivimey and Lachterman, 1980). Indeed, much of the case for TC is based on a negative critique of the oral-only approach.

Conrad, and a number of other people in Britain with similar views, believed that there was a clearcut case for the use of sign in the education of deaf children (Montgomery, 1980; Evans, 1982; British Deaf Association, 1985). Advocates of TC held that the oral approach was directly responsible for the low educational, linguistic and speech intelligibility standards typically achieved by deaf young people and, therefore, the oral approach had much to answer for. It was believed to be essential that an alternative approach be found in order to improve matters.

To strengthen their case TC advocates offer many reasons for the 'inevitable' failure of a purely oral approach. Normally hearing children use their hearing from the earliest days for language acquisition (Fry, 1977) and, therefore, when they start school aged 5 years they have a long history of language experience: deaf children, however, miss most of this experience. If children have hearing losses greater than 70 dB HL, they hear little or no speech before they are fitted with hearing aids. (The volume of normal conversational speech varies from around 50–70 dB.) Even when fitted with hearing aids profoundly deaf children at first hear only faint noises. So, whether or not the profoundly deaf child eventually masters spoken language, by the age of three, he or she may have little or no expressive verbal language. This contrasts with the normally hearing 3-year-old who typically has a vocabulary of around 1000 words and is using language internally to support thinking (Aitchison, 1989). Thus, it is argued, the profoundly deaf child, as well as having limited communication, suffers a cognitive and a linguistic deficit in the early years of life (Conrad, 1979).

Advocates of TC acknowledge that a few deaf children, despite this setback, will go on to develop verbal language from an oral approach and will, to use Conrad's term, develop 'inner speech': an internal representation of speech. However, it is argued that for most deaf children the auditory information coming from the speech environment is so degraded by the hearing loss that it cannot represent an analogue of speech. The acoustic elements of speech are not distinguished well enough to support an internal representation of spoken language: too many speech sounds 'sound alike'. TC advocates emphasise that the deaf child's ability to perceive the grammatical features of English is particularly restricted. In English, it is the syntactical elements which are the hardest to perceive through audition: function words, such as *a, the, as, of, to*, are very short and in 'running speech', unstressed. The inflexions, such as *ed*, at the end of a verb or *s*, as a plural or possessive, are generally fleeting and acoustically weak.

Hearing aids rectify some aspects of the hearing deficit but, according to the TC view, they cannot compensate for the discrimination difficulties caused by the damaged auditory system. Moreover, hearing aids amplify the entire auditory environment: they cannot do what the normal ear can do which is to discriminate speech signals from background noise. Hence, the speech perception difficulties of the deaf child are compounded.

Furthermore, it is argued that it is not possible to perceive speech through lipreading. The information offered by lipreading is generally agreed to be limited: many sounds of speech look alike on the lips, e.g. *p, b, m,*; some sounds are invisible, e.g. *k, g, n,*; and in 'running speech' most vowels are very hard to differentiate. Speech needs to be *heard* to be perceived: seeing speech is not enough.

That a minority of what are believed to be exceptional deaf children can overcome the 'sound barrier' is insufficient, according to the TC argument, to justify an educational approach which condemns the majority to an impossible or at best very arduous struggle to acquire language through the aural medium. With an auditory-oral approach, they say, the deaf child acquires vocabulary slowly and laboriously. It is further argued that there is no way at present of predicting which deaf children will be successful with the oral-only approach. That argument, coupled with the belief that the early use of signs does not negatively affect the deaf child's chance of acquiring good speech (Freeman, Carbin and Boese, 1981), means that there is no justification for withholding signs as a readily available means of communication to the developing deaf child.

In addition, advocates of TC do not hold as positive a view as oralists of the capacity of hearing aids to effectively exploit the deaf child's residual hearing. They do not share the oralist belief that with good amplification, the deaf child can receive sufficient auditory information to develop verbal language. So, despite technological advances in amplification, TC supporters believe that most deaf* children are simply too deaf to perceive spoken language through the auditory channel alone. They believe that the use of signs, far from detracting from the auditory experience, will fruitfully supplement a pure oral approach. The oral approach, it is argued, has failed many deaf children in the past and, therefore, a sensible alternative, one which can offer language in a more readily accessible form, is required if deaf children are not going to continue to be 'failed' in the future.

The case for TC does not just rest, however, on the 'failure' of pure oralism. Advocates of TC offer several positive reasons for believing that TC will be more effective in offering language and communication to the deaf child.

To consider first the use of TC during the pre-school years: the effort for parents of learning sign is more than repaid, so it is claimed, by having much easier and, therefore, more satisfying communication with the developing deaf child (Thompson and Swisher, 1985). The young deaf child will readily use gestures and signs and through their use he or she will be able to respond to the communicative overtures of caregivers. By the use of signs in addition to speech, interaction with the deaf child is not inhibited by difficulties of communication. It is believed that without the pressure to communicate solely by oral means, paradoxically, the deaf child will vocalise and verbalise *more* freely than with a purely auditory-oral approach (Norden, 1981). By being allowed to use sign and gesture the deaf child learns how to communicate in a normal and relaxed way. The deaf child who is permitted, indeed encouraged, to communicate with means other than speech develops confidence and with confidence even the difficult task of using speech becomes more of a possibility. By the use of signs, according to this argument, the process of language acquisition is accelerated and is much more likely to follow the time-scale of language acquisition of normally hearing children (Schlesinger and Meadow, 1972).

Furthermore, it is claimed that TC has a positive effect on the deaf child's emotional development and avoids the psychologically harmful effects caused by an oral-only approach. Making use of signs by caregivers in the early years ensures effective bonding between care-giver and deaf child and encourages, much more easily than speech alone, the development of an emotionally close relationship (Meadow, 1980).

So, for parents, the task of communicating and bringing language to

---

*Those who believe in the need to use signs with speech with deaf children tend not to specify what they mean by 'deaf'. It is probably that in the UK, where TC is used as a matter of policy with deaf children, the child's hearing loss is likely to be 90 dB or greater. Many supporters of TC would probably consider children with hearing losses less than 90 dB as having sufficient hearing for the development of speech through audition.

the young deaf child is considered to be made easier by the use of signs. The same is said to be true for teachers. Where signs can be used in the classroom it is believed to be easier to convey information, teach new vocabulary and simply communicate more effectively; the break-downs of communication and the restrictions of language that have been observed in oral-only classrooms (Ivimey, 1981; Wood et al., 1986), are avoided.

A TC approach can observe the same principle of using natural language as is generally recommended with the auditory-oral approach. The advantage of TC, so it is claimed, is that it is much *easier* to talk naturally where signs can support the conveying of meaning. Conversational exchange is not held up by misunderstandings, repetition and repair work, so that teachers can communicate spontaneously in a relaxed and non-controlling way. The development of literacy can also be helped by the use of signs to decode and encode the written word. Indeed, throughout the school years, advocates of TC claim that signs form an invaluable teaching tool in providing easy access to new knowledge, new concepts and new vocabulary. Where deaf children are being educated in ordinary schools, support teachers or assistants in the mainstream classes can, through the use of signs offered at appropriate times during the lesson, explain difficult items offered by the class teacher – and without any disturbance to the rest of the class! Generally, TC is held to improve access for the deaf child to a broad and balanced curriculum.

To summarise: TC is justified as the proper educational approach because it makes use of the visual medium for conveying linguistic symbols, including the grammatical features of verbal language. TC is believed to provide 'total' information, whereas the oral-only approach offers 'partial' information. With improved access to linguistic symbols the process of language acquisition is accelerated, and the deaf child has readier access to knowledge of all kinds. Inevitably, so it is argued, the educational standards of deaf children will be raised with the adoption of the TC principle and the TC practice. If the claims can in practice be met a TC approach offers the deaf child: easy communication, spoken language, the ability to read and write, and the ability to use sign fluently when in the company of other deaf children and adults. TC is thus seen to offer the 'best of all worlds'.

An Evaluation of TC

As with the case for oralism many of the arguments used to support TC, persuasive and appealing though they may be, are based on what, from a 'common sense' point of view seems reasonable and on what, 'in theory', seems plausible. Whilst from a 'common sense' point of view the TC approach seems logical and desirable, regrettably, 'common sense' does not always turn out to be correct: it is necessary to look at research evidence on the efficiency of TC as a means of communication and to examine the evidence of the attainments of TC educated children in order to evaluate the claims.

Crucial to the TC case, given that verbal language is the goal, is that the use of signs by a deaf child, in particular in the early years, does not detract from the development of spoken language and does not reduce the capacity of the hearing mechanisms to receive important linguistic information through audition. TC advocates have frequently cited evidence from the past, usually from the USA, of studies involving deaf children of deaf parents (DCDP) to support their case. According to these studies DCDP have been shown to achieve better educational standards and higher attainments in speech and language than deaf children with similar hearing losses who have hearing parents (DCHP) (Quigley and Frisina, 1961; Stuckless and Birch, 1966; Meadow, 1968). It was therefore concluded, assuming the children of deaf parents used sign in the home, that not only does sign language not detract from the development of spoken communication, it actually enhances oral development and improves academic attainments.

These findings and the interpretation of them have, however, been criticised. In the first place we are not told about the nature of the signing that was used in the homes of the DCDP (Quigley and Paul, 1984); if natural sign, such as ASL, was used then this provides little support for a combined system of signs and speech *per se*. Secondly, explanations other than the early use of sign have been offered to account for the advantage of DCDP over DCHP. For example, some research by Corson (1973) compares the achievements of deaf children of speech-using deaf parents with deaf children of sign-using deaf parents. The results indicate that the children of speech-using deaf parents outperformed the children of sign-using deaf parents on linguistic, speech intelligibility, and other educational measures. This evidence suggests that it is something other than the early use of sign which is giving the DCDP their advantage. Corson suggests that DCDP have the advantage of being much more easily accepted by parents as *deaf* children than is the case with DCHP where it can take some time for hearing parents to adjust emotionally to having a deaf child. Thirdly, the oral standards achieved by *all* the deaf children who featured in the US studies were low when compared to those of the school population as a whole. Given that the attainments were so poor overall, that the DCDP were marginally ahead linguistically and educationally does not overwhelmingly commend the use of sign in the development of verbal language. Finally, the documentation on the deaf children involved in these studies is scant and we are not given information about all the many factors which might influence the oral attainments of the deaf children, e.g. age of diagnosis, use of hearing aids, communication approach used at school, etc. (Quigley and Kretschmer, 1982). This means that it is very difficult to interpret the findings and draw any firm conclusions from them as to whether the early use of sign does or does not detract from the development of spoken language.

If TC is to be judged as an effective means of delivering language to deaf children then there has to be some examination of the practice of TC, that is, of explicit attempts to use both speech and signs in combination. Given that TC has been widely used for the last 20 years, in particular in the USA, then it should be possible to make some evaluation of TC. Some reports have been positive: they relate mainly to the linguistic progress of younger deaf children and tend to be based on experience of TC use in the 1970s rather than the 1980s. We will start with some examples from the USA.

Schlesinger and Meadow (1972), examined the language acquisition of three deaf children who had been exposed from an early age (15 months to 3 years) to a form of Signed English. These three children were reported to have made more rapid progress with syntax and vocabulary than is normally found with deaf children on an oral-only approach. The children were acquiring grammatical competence in the same sequence as hearing children though at a slower rate. The numbers involved here are small and the degree of parental interest and support great. However, this is not to detract from the fact that these young deaf children, in the early stages of language acquisition, were succeeding linguistically with a TC approach.

A study which examined the linguistic progress of a larger group of deaf children was undertaken by Bornstein, Saulnier and Hamilton (1980). There were 20 4-year-old prelingually deaf children in the sample with a mean hearing loss of 88 dB. The children were studied over a period of four years. The children were evaluated each year for four years by use of tests of syntax and vocabulary. The children were instructed in speech and Signed English by their teachers. Parents also made attempts to communicate simultaneously in SE and speech with the children. The standards of SE of the parents was not high: most of the mothers achieved competencies between an average and beginner's level and most fathers did not get beyond the beginner's stage. However, the results showed that, at the end of the four-year period, the vocabulary level of the children was similar to the vocabulary of deaf children three years older. Their rate of growth of receptive vocabulary was roughly 43% of that observed in hearing children. The growth of their skill in reception of syntactic markers was similar to that of hearing children, and the children did not stop using their voices as a result of using simultaneous communication. Again, this evidence suggests that not only is there no reason not to use TC in the early years but that SE in a TC approach can offer better results than are usually reported for young deaf children.

A much-cited study by Brasel and Quigley (1977), also in the USA, investigated the effects of intensity and type of early language and communication approach on the later linguistic achievements of deaf pupils. Four groups were studied: one group involved deaf parents who had used Manual English with their deaf children in infancy and early childhood; a second group involved deaf parents who used ASL with their deaf children; a third group had hearing parents who employed an intensive oral approach in infancy and early childhood and a fourth group involved hearing parents who were not actively involved in the communication development of their deaf children. The findings from the three groups of deaf children who had experienced a specific approach in the early years revealed a significant superiority of the Manual English group on nearly all of the language and communication measures. The ASL and intensive oral group were about the same. The fourth group who probably received neither sign input nor intensive oral input in the home were significantly below the other three groups in their communication attainments.

The findings from the Brasel and Quigley study demonstrate the important point that when judging an approach it is not necessarily the approach *per se* that underlies achievements but the enthusiasm and dedication associated with the implementation of that approach. However, if it can be assumed that the approaches used with the three 'intensive' groups were equally efficiently implemented then this research offers some support for the superiority of Signed English for giving deaf children language and communication.

An example of some European evaluation of TC comes from Scandinavia. Norden (1981), reporting from Sweden, presents a study of pre-school profoundly deaf children who were enrolled at a kindergarten attended by both deaf and normally hearing children. Signed Swedish was used by all the staff and by some of the hearing children. Since the hearing children were in the majority there was much spoken language in the deaf children's environment. No pressure was put on the young deaf children to vocalise or verbalise. It was observed that there was an overall acceleration in the language development of the deaf children after attending the kindergarten. This was believed to be a direct consequence of being 'allowed to use communicative symbols that they could easily perceive and produce, (Norden, 1981). When the deaf children began reading activities they spontaneously used speech, voiced or voiceless articulations of the words in the book. Thus, concludes the author, it is clear that TC in no way inhibited the development of speech and may in fact have facilitated it.

Some recent research in the UK indicates that gesture and sign have a constructive role to play in the deaf child's progression to vocal symbolisation, but only in the early stages of communication development (Robinshaw, 1992). The transition from non-communicative behaviour to language production was examined in five chronologically and culturally matched pairs of deaf and hearing infants. All the deaf infants were early diagnosed and were using hearing aids by age six months. The children were studied at regular intervals up to the age of 21 months. Robinshaw found that deaf and hearing infants followed the same sequence of development from non-communicative behaviour to single-word speech, but that with one exception, the deaf infants were delayed relative to the hearing infants. For all the infants, deaf and hearing, the use of communicative gesture formed an important step from pre-symbolic to symbolic language. The hearing infants' use of gesture declined markedly beyond the age of 12 months when first words were emerging. The deaf children's use of gesture declined only towards the end of the period of study as their auditory perception improved and their vocalisations became more intelligible to care-givers. The author concluded that the use of gesture\signs as well as vocalisation promotes mutual communication between deaf child and care-giver at a time when interpreting the vocalisations of the deaf child is difficult. She speculates, however, that the continued use of gesture\sign by care-givers would have a detrimental effect on the development of auditory discrimination and vocal\verbal communication.

A study coming from the UK provides some encouragement for the use of TC with deaf children during their school years. Evans (1989) looked at the perceptions of parents of the influence of a TC approach on the education of their children. Parents of 100 deaf children who had changed from a pure oral approach to a TC approach gave their views on the effects of TC on their child's use of residual hearing, speech and lipreading ability, emotional and social development and on language and educational growth. Most of the children were profoundly deaf: the mean age was 12;2, the average age up to which oral comunication was used was 7;2, and the average number of years of TC use was 4 years 9 months. The findings indicated that, in the views of the parents, the children did not make less use of their hearing aids after TC nor did they use less speech. Indeed, the majority of parents reported improvements in their overall communication, including lipreading and speech. Most of the parents considered the use of TC had improved not only their children's language and educational growth but also their social and emotional development. Parents could, on the whole, understand their children better when they used signs as well as speech. Less than half of the parents could understand all or most of what their children communicated through speech alone but around 90% of parents could understand their children when signing and finger spelling were added. There was even more marked improvement in the children's understanding of their parents' communication when using speech and signs, with 94% of the children reported to understand all or most of the information given by their parents. Clearly, the parents featuring in the Evans study believed that TC was a useful innovation from several points of view. We do not have any objective measures of the communication abilities of the deaf children, before and after TC, and we cannot be sure, therefore, that the children were making better progress with TC than they would have done if they had remained on an oral-only approach.

The other kind of evidence held to be supportive of TC relates not to the overall linguistic attainments of children exposed to a TC approach but to the process of offering information through signs and speech. White and Stevenson (1975), and Grove and Rodda (1984), for example, compared four modes of communication of information presented to deaf secondary-age residential school pupils in the USA. The modes were oral-only, sign-only, TC, and reading. Both studies demonstrated a superiority of TC over oral-only presentation. Both, however, found reading to be the most successful in conveying information. The White and Stevenson study did not indicate any advantage of TC over the sign-only mode. So this research, though suggesting that TC may be more effective than speech alone in transmitting information to children and young people who have been educated in a 'signs and speech' environment, does not give strong support for signs and speech being the *most* effective means of offering information.

On the question of information transmission the picture is rather confusing. Goetzinger (1978), cites research which investigated the effects of varying combinations of communication modes: lipreading and audition; lipreading, audition and signs; and lipreading and signs, on a sample of 8–10-year-old deaf children. Where signs and lipreading were available together it was noted that the children either attempted to lipread or they followed the signs: they did not do both. Goetzinger (1978) concludes:

> the organism cannot process two visual signals simultaneously. One or the other would become essentially noise and hence would either be suppressed or ignored (p.455).

Where auditory amplification was used in combination with the two visual media there was again, according to the research, no evidence of mutual support and reinforcement of the information received through the different media. Goetzinger believes that the sounds of speech and lip patterns of speech are mutually compatible and together they facilitate the reception of spoken language. Any form of signing, however, represents a symbol system which is incompatible with speech and, therefore, the two systems of communication are not mutually reinforcing.

The interpretation of Goetzinger (1978) that speech and signs do not go together is challenged by Wood and Wood (1992b). Their in-depth study of five deaf children using TC suggests that signs and speech are a 'package' for communication purposes and not two separate codes. They say the two modes go together and the children seemed to need to use them together. They claim it did not appear to be beyond the cognitive capacity of the children to attend to signs and speech together.

It could be argued that it does not really matter whether or not signs plus speech aid communication in the here-and-now, and that their joint use may be preferred by deaf children who have had exposure to a TC approach is not the issue: what does matter is the extent to which TC contributes to language acquisition and the development of spoken and written language.

The research already cited, which indicated a superiority of TC over oral-only methods for language acquisition and later language development, and which provided such impetus to the adoption of TC policies in schools, has in more recent years come under a great deal of attack. Indeed, many ardent TC advocates of the late 1970s became, a decade later, some of the fiercest critics of the TC approach (Hansen, 1991). Methodologies have been criticised largely on the grounds that the several variables which can influence deaf children's achievements have not been sufficiently taken into account (Quigley and Paul, 1984). For example, the so-called oral-only children who featured in the studies cited, were almost certainly not on a pure oral approach. Quigley and Kretschmer (1982) inform us that many samples of 'orally educated' children were 'at best' only exposed to oral communication in the classroom. We have no specific information about the different kinds of communication experience of the TC educated children nor whether there was consistency of mode of communication between home and school. Moreover, much of the evidence concerns the language development of young children in the relatively early stages of acquisition and does not tell us anything about their subsequent verbal language attainments.

That we should be cautious about our interpretation of the findings which indicate that TC accelerates language acquisition is indicated by a follow-up study undertaken by Bornstein and Saulnier (1981). The children when aged 9–10 years, that is one year after the main study, were assessed for their use of Signed English markers. A 'slight improvement' was indicated, but the rate of improvement had slowed down. This finding could, according to the authors, be interpreted as 'disappointing'. It led to the conclusion that further exploration of how best to use manual systems to facilitate the learning of English was 'still very much in order'.

It is easy to condemn research findings of investigations into the achievements of deaf children given the number and complexity of the variables involved. However, the criticisms of the early research on TC seem entirely justified when the large-scale surveys of TC educated children are examined. The greatest condemnation of all the condemnations of TC, at least of the way it is currently practised, is that TC educated young people are achieving no higher standards of verbal language than deaf children were before the introduction of TC. Data, based on the 1982-3 'Annual Survey of Hearing-Impaired Children and Youth' from the Center for Assessment and Demographic Studies, Gallaudet Research Institute, for example, revealed that the average reading age of profoundly deaf school leavers in the USA was between 3rd and 4th grade, that is, between 8 and 9 years (Allen, 1986). A sample of 2414 children and young people of all ages was assessed for speech intelligibility. Overall, 55% were judged to have 'unintelligible' or 'barely intelligible' speech (Wolk and Schildroth, 1986). At the time of the Gallaudet survey 86% of profoundly deaf children and young people were in TC programmes and had been for all or most of their school lives. The survey findings are no different from those reported by the Babbidge Committee in 1965 in the USA and by Conrad in 1979 in the UK on the standards achieved by deaf children *before* the TC innovation.

Moreover, more recent research which examines the relative achievements of TC and orally educated children reveals a superiority in both speech attainments and command of English by the orally educated children. Geers, Moog and Schick (1984) investigated the achievements of 327 profoundly deaf children from oral-auditory (OA) and TC programmes from across the USA. Each child had been educated with consistent communication, either OA *or* TC, since the age of three. The children were tested on their production of selected English language structures. The results were analysed for four different response modes: oral production of the OA children; oral production of TC children; sign production of TC children; and combined production of TC children.

The findings were: the scores of the OA children were higher than the sign or combined production of the TC children in over 50% of the grammatical categories; the sign scores of the TC children were above the scores of the OA children in less than 20% of the grammatical categories; the oral productions of the TC children were below their own sign and combined scores and below the scores of the OA children in all grammatical categories. The gap between the oral and sign production of the TC children indicates that spoken English does not develop simultaneously with signed English. The gap between the production of the OA and TC children indicates that children exposed to a signed form of English do not develop competence with English at a rate faster than those not using signs.

A recent UK study compared the speech intelligibility of orally educated and TC educated children over a period of 5 years (Markides,

1988). The children were all aged 10 years at the start of the study. Markides found that over that period the speech intelligibility of the oral children improved significantly but that the speech intelligibility of the TC children deteriorated significantly. The author concluded that the TC children came to rely less and less on use of their hearing for speech and were less and less likely to use speech for communication purposes.

So, where later linguistic achievements are examined, the overall standards of TC educated children are low when compared with those of normally hearing children and low when compared with those deaf children on 'incontestably oral programmes' (Quigley and Kretschmer, 1982). The research examined seems to suggest that if signs are used *early* in the deaf child's life, then they may promote the development of verbal communication at the initial stages, but that if the use of signs persist, then the deaf child relies more and more on signs to the detriment of the development of use of residual hearing and of spoken language.

It is interesting and significant that during the 1980s, corresponding with the reports of low attainments of TC educated children, more and more research has emerged which demonstrates problems with both the principles and the practice of TC.

Several researchers have looked at TC from the point of view of presentation. When TC was originally conceived it was believed to be possible 'to present simultaneously signed and spoken information with full respect to English syntax' (Denton, 1976). However, the findings of Baker (1978), and other investigators, Marmor and Petitto (1979) and Strong and Charlson (1987) suggest that this is *intrinsically* an impossible task. Baker (1978), for example, observes that the rate of articulation of speech alone is approximately twice the rate of manual English signs alone. The user of SE who is simultaneously using speech must somehow resolve this rate differential. Baker's research, involving 14 skilled signers with 18–40 years' experience, indicated that attempts to deal with the rate differential problem had a deleterious effect on the presentation of both signs and speech. She reported that when using sim-com her subjects not only markedly decreased their speaking rate but also, because still speaking much faster than they were signing, deleted much important information from their signed component.

Baker's findings, that the spoken signal or the signed message or both suffer in sim-com, have been confirmed many times over the last decade or so (Marmor and Petitto, 1979; Kluwin, 1981; Huntington and Watton, 1984a,b; Newton, 1985; Lynas, Huntington and Tucker, 1988). Typically, the speech accompanying the signs is slowed down and altered phonologically: vowels and diphthongs become elongated and gaps in speaking occur so that the oral delivery becomes halting and hesitant. The normal rhythm of English is distorted and so also is the normal relationship between vowels and consonants (Lynas, Huntington and Tucker, 1988). The maintenance of a normal relationship between the elements of speech has been shown many times to contribute significantly to speech intelligibility (Hudgins and Numbers, 1942; John and Howarth, 1965).

Signs in sim-com suffer not from distortion but from omission. Characteristically, the sim-com presenter will omit signs randomly or delete signs which do not fit the rhythmic pattern of English speech and\or delete the function words and inflexions of English (Baker 1978; Johnson, Liddell and Erting, 1989; Wood and Wood, 1992a). Wood and Wood (1992a), on the basis of their recent study of the use of SE in some English classrooms, comment:

> It is, we suspect, more than a cruel irony of fate that we have found that those aspects of English grammar and structure which deaf children find so difficult are also the least likely to appear in Signed English. It seems that those aspects of speech which are the most fleeting and which are acoustically, motorically and visually among the least salient, are also the most difficult to articulate with the hands (p. 13).

Some examples of signs and speech used in sim-com illustrating particularly the deletion of English morphological features are provided by Johnson, Liddell and Erting (1989). The investigators examined the SE and speech productions of a hearing pre-school teacher interacting with 4-year-old deaf children. The spoken English is in italics; sign glosses are in the upper case:

TELL   SAY   HORSE RABBIT   NO
Tell   tell the Easter Bunny   He said, No, he's

  FORGET TELL   THANK-YOU
You forgot to say you've say thank   you

ZERO ORANGE   SORRY   OUTSIDE ORANGE PICK OTHER COLOR
No orange. He's sorry but he's out of orange. Pick another color (p. 6).

On the basis of these observations and those of other researchers in the USA, the authors conclude:

> In our view, it is not an exaggeration to say that the signed portion of the SSS (Sign Supported Speech) presented in virtually all of American deaf education is only partially comprehensible, even to skilled native signers. It is also not an exaggeration to say that often the signed portion of the SSS in American classrooms is largely unintelligible (p. 5).

Johnson, Liddell and Erting (1989), however, may be overstating the case. It is perhaps not fair to take transcripts of signs and speech and present them 'out of context'. The meaning of the communication may have been a lot clearer to the children given all the situational clues. However, these examples of the signing which accompanies speech in sim-com show little evidence of 'full respect to English syntax'. The signs fall very far short of fulfilling the objective of bringing English grammar to deaf children in a readily accessible manual–visual form. Hence, the signing which is associated with speech in sim-com, whatever the nomenclature, inevitably becomes like SSE in that it represents only part of what is said. Baker (1978) concluded that to think what you are going to say and think about how you are going to encode it in the two different channels of speech and sign is intrinsically unmanageable. She refers to the problem of 'cognitive overload' and suggests that, inevitably, there will be a slowing down of transmission rate and deletion of signs.

Lack of grammaticity is not all that goes wrong with signing in a TC approach. Kluwin (1981), based on his observations in classrooms in the USA, offers several reasons why the signs of SE or SSE cannot, or do not, match the accompanying speech. He points out that SE is based on written English which does not always conform to the conventions of everyday colloquial English. For example, *'I gonna ...'* is acceptable (in the USA) when spoken but the utterance cannot be signed except by *'I am going to ....* Pitch and pacing cannot be easily represented nor can intonation. A linguistically important feature of spoken English is that a statement can be made into a question or a command simply by changing the intonation pattern. For example, *'You are going home'*, *'You are going home?'*, *'You are going home!'*.

Idiom is particularly difficult to translate from spoken to signed English because of the iconic or pictographic nature of many signs. Kluwin gives the example of the sign gloss for the 'running' of *'My nose is running'* as the action of 'running' as an athlete might. This clearly, he claims, is a semantic violation and he cites many more examples of semantic distortion in his article (Kluwin, 1981).

The research of Newton (1985), also conducted in the USA, confirms the difficulty for teachers, using TC, in representing figurative language in the signed version of English. She notes that language in use is highly idiomatic. For example, *'take a bath'*,*'turn out the light'*, *'eat up'*. Non-literal language such as this cannot 'word for word' be translated into another language. Her investigation involved 30 teacher\child dyads: 10 teachers with hearing children; 10 teachers using an auditory-oral approach with deaf children and 10 teachers using TC with deaf children. The hearing children were aged between 2;4 and 3;0. The deaf children were older, aged from 5;11 and 9;3. All the teachers had had much previous interaction with the children. The teachers were observed in spontaneous communication, talking about objects in the room, and in a story-telling activity. The teachers of the hearing children and the auditory-oral teachers were found to be similar in their use of idiom. Around 20% of their utterances contained at least one idiomatic usage. The TC teachers made much less use of idiom in their speech. Where the TC teachers did use idiomatic language in their speech 60% was not signed. There was no non-literal signing that was not spoken. So the TC promise of 'full presentation of language in all its richness' is not fulfilled, if this research finding can be generalised.

Newton's evidence suggests that teachers using a TC approach, whether consciously or not, restrict what they say to avoid difficulties of translating what they say into sign. Other evidence confirms that the spoken component of TC is simpler and less varied than when speech is used without signs. A UK study by Huntington and Watton (1984a,b) examined the spoken language of teachers in special schools and units, some of whom were using a TC approach, the others an oral-only approach. The research indicated that the TC teachers offered less enriched language and less academic stimulus in comparison with oral-only teachers. Teachers using TC produced shorter and less grammatically complex spoken utterances, used a more restricted vocabulary, posed fewer 'open' questions, and provided 30–40% less in terms of lesson content. In view of the fact that teachers of the deaf in the UK do not receive specialist training in signing, unlike their American counterparts, it is tempting to conclude that British teachers may be restricting their spoken language when using TC in order to be able to match what they say to the signs that they know. If it is the case that many teachers using TC restrict their spoken language input, then this may explain why the oral achievements of TC educated children are as low as they are.

Some observers of practice in TC schools and classrooms offer a further explanation for poor speech and spoken language attainments (Potts, 1974; Latimer, 1983). Potts (1974), for example, observing a combined method of signing and talking in special schools in Copenhagen, reports that too little attention was paid to the use of the children's residual hearing and relatively too much attention was paid to developing signing ability. This was despite the fact that the children were provided with very good hearing aids.

Latimer (1983), reporting TC practice in schools for the deaf in the Mid-West part of the USA, was 'shocked, surprised and dismayed' at what he saw in relation to the development of spoken communication. Based on his observations of teachers in classrooms he reported: the production of words without voice; 'a lamentable lack of knowledge by the teacher' of how to use amplification equipment; broken amplification equipment; a belief on the part of teachers that 'speech is something done by a specialist speech therapist for 15 minutes a day or every other day or once a week'. His conclusion was that TC was very far from 'total' and that 'good TC skills' had come to mean simply signing proficiency.

An investigation by Lai and Lynas (1991) supports the finding of Huntington and Watton (1984a,b) that the signing of TC teachers can be very far from proficient. The research was undertaken in Hong Kong and compared the interactions between teachers of the deaf and their pupils, each over a period of 10 minutes, using different communication approaches: oral, cued-speech* and TC. The teachers using TC had received little or no training in signing. No matter which approach was used neither the teachers nor the children were judged to be using 'normal' language. There were however, distinctive features of communication associated with the TC teachers: they signed only a little of what they said; there was a definite bias towards signing content words and an almost complete absence of function words and morphological features of English; the range of signed vocabulary was very restricted. The findings were as follows:

Eighty-seven point six per cent of what was signed were nouns or verbs

Five verbs (translated into English) represented 84% of all the verbs which were signed – like, dislike, eat, know, forget

Five nouns represented 92% of nouns signed – mother, grandmother, uncle, brother, sister

Five adjectives represented 100% of the adjectives signed – many, delicious, small, long, big.

These results suggest that these teachers signed a few words rather a lot. The authors concluded that the teachers:

did not, therefore, seem to be using signs for the purpose of conveying more rapidly and easily new or difficult vocabulary. On the contrary, it was for the more common and familiar words that signs were offered (Lai and Lynas, 1991, p. 250).

The studies reviewed, based on observations of TC in classrooms, suggest variations in practice. These variations are probably related to the differences in signing competence of the teachers. But even where teachers are good signers the aim of TC to fully exploit all modes of communication and deliver enriched and complex language is not, so it would appear, being fulfilled.

---

*Cued speech involves manual representation of phonetic elements of speech that are not readily visible for speech reading. This approach is not examined in this work because so rarely used with deaf children in the UK. Readers wishing to learn more about the approach are advised to read Cornett, 1967. Information can also be obtained from: The National Centre for Cued Speech for the Deaf, 29–30 Watling Street, Canterbury CT1 2UD, UK.

So far we have been considering the problems with TC from the point of view of the presenter. As we have already seen, there may be some question as to whether deaf children can follow signs, listen and lipread at the same time (Goetzinger, 1978). A less equivocal finding reported recently relates to the necessity of the receiver of the signed message being in the line of sight of the sender (Matthews and Reich, 1993). Children in school spend much time on activities (for example, practical tasks, looking at books, worksheets, blackboard, computers, etc.) which necessitate focusing away from the teacher and away from other pupils. It could be hypothesised, therefore, that because of the problem of divided attention deaf school pupils might miss some of the messages that are signed to them. The study by Matthews and Reich, (1993) confirms that this is the case. They videotaped segments of lessons in secondary TC classes for the deaf in the USA and observed that on average the signed messages sent by teachers and students were seen less than half the time. The researchers concluded that for information transfer: 'the constraints of line-of-sight communication are profound'.

Further critical comment, however, comes from an examination of the use children make of the signs that they do receive in order to communicate spontaneously. There is accumulating evidence that deaf children exposed to TC do not use Signed English when communicating amongst themselves. Gee and Goodhart (1988), for example, observing deaf children in the USA exposed to some form of Manually Coded English, note that the children in spontaneous communication do not use English in signed form but 'innovate forms that are more or less like those of ASL even without ASL input'. This finding is confirmed by several other American writers (Suty and Friel-Patty, 1982; Livingstone, 1983; Evans and Falk, 1986). Similarly, Hansen (1990), referring to the Danish experience of TC reports of TC educated children that:

> their Danish did not improve ... and they continued to communicate amongst themselves and with deaf adults in a sign system completely different from the one their hearing parents and teachers used to them – a system the teachers and parents could not understand (p. 2).

An explanation for this phenomenon is that where signs are used by children for 'real' communication there is a strong tendency, obligation even, to 'nativise', that is, to bring the signs into a language structure which is natural to signed communication. Regular use of signs with other sign users more or less compels the child sign user to develop structures which are adapted to natural sign language. The structure of English when artificially formulated in the medium of sign appears to violate the 'rules' of 'genuine' sign language and runs counter to what should 'naturally' develop during the process of sign language acquisition. What happens when young deaf children are exposed to English sign is likened to the 'nativisation' process that occurs when young children are exposed to pidgin (Gee and Goodhart, 1988). Pidgin is a rudimentary form of language devised for communication purposes by people who do not share a language in common. Pidgin is 'telegraphic' in form, that is, it has 'content' words but lacks grammatical structures and is thereby distinguished from 'true' languages. Remarkably, however, young children exposed to pidgin do not persist in the use of 'telegraphese' but take the words of pidgin and create syntactical features, that is, they add structure and develop a real language, a process known as creolization (Bickerton, 1981). The deaf child, similarly so it is suggested, takes the signs presented in the form of English and adds the morphological features of 'true' sign language.

If it is the case that the deaf child 'nativises' when exposed to Signed English then this in itself offers an explanation for the failure of TC approaches to bring English grammar to the deaf. Exposure to Signed English may serve the deaf child in encouraging the development of natural sign language but it does little for the acquisition of English.

The current attack on TC comes from many directions. The oralists have always been of the opinion that adding sign to the spoken word would not only not benefit the deaf child's language development but would probably detract from the acquisition of spoken language and the ability to use residual hearing to good effect. Oralists, therefore, feel vindicated in their views. But also many people, who were supportive of TC because of the introduction of sign into the education of deaf children, now condemn TC. Some citations from individuals who were initially supportive of TC and who continue to believe that sign should be used in the education of deaf children illustrate the 'chorus of disapproval':

> Our research has yielded surprising and unsettling results that Simultaneous Communication as it is currently used in schools, may do little to bring English grammar to deaf children (Marmor and Petitto, 1979, p. 125).

> Overall, however, total communication, with its myriad of definitions and as presently carried out, has not had the hoped for effects in large-scale studies (Schlesinger, 1986, p. 108).

> Since the 1970s, most deaf children have been educated in Total Communication programs in which some form of signing and speech is used simultaneously for communication and instructional purposes. Despite improvement in the development of tests, early amplification, and the implementation of early intervention or preschool programs, most students are still functionally illiterate upon graduation from high school (Paul, 1988, p. 3).

> ... the validity of the underlying assumption that any system of signs (either natural or invented) is capable of representing speech in a way which will allow it to serve as a model for the natural acquisition of a spoken language has never been demonstrated (Johnson, Liddell and Erting, 1989, p. 8).

On the subject of change, Wendy Daunt had good news from Derby. In September 1990, The Royal School for the Deaf will drop the 'Total Communication' (or, in Wendy's words, Total Confusion) label in favour of bilingualism ... Why did Derby decide to change? Wendy looked at the effect of 'TC' on children's achievements in school. She found no improvement in their communication, education, BSL, English, oral skills, social skills or reading age (BDA, 1990).

This condemnation stems in part from the overall failure of TC to raise the educational standard of deaf individuals and in part because the aims of TC are too similar to those of oralism. The aim of TC, to bring *English* language to deaf children as a top priority, is seen by many as 'crypto-oralism' (Johnson, Liddell and Erting, 1989). In increasing numbers, educators, academics and deaf people themselves believe that it is time to look again at the nature and role of sign language in the education of deaf children (Paul, 1987; Christensen, 1989; O'Rourke, 1990; Stewart, 1990; Pickersgill 1991).

The Future of TC

So at the moment TC, at least according to current rhetoric, is having a 'hard time'. TC is not completely without supporters, however. There has been recent defence of bi-modal presentation and of the signing of verbal language. Maxwell (1990), for example, challenges the idea that manually coded English is ungrammatical and largely unintelligible. She acknowledges the inherent difficulties of signing *exact* English simultaneously with speech. She accepts that there will inevitably be deletions of morphological features in the signed component. However, she suggests that the fact that sign and speech channels do not exactly correspond does not mean that what is signed gives no representation of English at all. Based on some observations of informal classroom conversations in sim-com between hearing teachers and deaf high school students (Maxwell, 1985), she reports that the structure of the English sentence was preserved in the signed portion, albeit in a more skeletal form. That the deaf students were signing to their teachers using English-like structures is evidence that features of English are made available through sim-com.

Maxwell cites the frequently reported observation that when deaf signers communicate with hearing signers it is through English-type signing and when with other deaf people they communicate through natural sign-type signing (Johnson and Erting, 1989; Gustason, 1990). That is, deaf signing people typically code-switch from manual forms of verbal language to natural sign and vice versa depending on the context. That deaf individuals exposed to sim-com are adept at both is indicated by some research by Eagney (1987). His study involved children and young people from a day school for the deaf in the USA where manually coded English was used in the classroom. Information was presented in three communication modes: ASL, simplified manual English, and standard manual English. He reported no significant difference in comprehension related to communication mode.

Manually-coded English is, therefore, according to Maxwell (1990), not only accessible to the deaf but also, in certain contexts, constitutes a valid form of communication. She argues also that the research which just looks at the grammaticality of signing in bi-modal presentation misses a lot of what is going on from a communication point of view. She suggests that there is a relationship between what is signed and what is spoken and that the synergy between the two channels does contribute to the overall intelligibility of the message. The omission of signed tokens of English morphemes does not necessarily lead to 'drastic semantic difficulty' and what is deleted may be recoverable from the context. She believes that when making judgements about communicative effectiveness it is essential to examine the *whole* context in the conversational setting. Maxwell (1990) concludes:

> In essence it is not at all an inevitable conclusion that the use of bimodal language presents incoherent, unintelligible or confusing input to receivers (p. 343).

Maxwell, along with a number of other writers and commentators, continues to believe in the value of bi-modal communication given that it is done 'properly' (Thompson and Swisher, 1985; Gaustad, 1986; Ritter-Brinton, 1990). This undoubtedly means improving on much of current practice and developing greater fluency in bi-modal production. Some research in the USA, involving deaf students at college, provides evidence that not only is it possible to present information effectively through sim-com but it is also possible to distinguish 'good' sim-com presenters from 'bad' ones (Mallery-Ruganis, Wilkins and Fischer, 1990).

Given the assumption that some deaf children need some signing in order to communicate and develop language it is, so some educators would claim, more realistic to work towards improving bi-modal communication rather than abandoning the TC approach in favour of the relatively new, untried and untested option of bilingualism. Most educators of the deaf in the UK and the USA who use sign are probably unlikely to readily abandon an approach which they can understand and which they are trying to implement to greater effect.

Whether or not an improved version of TC will develop in the future remains to be seen. Whether it will be considered ethically and politically legitimate to continue to use a form of signing manipulated to conform to English rules is a crucial issue. In the present social and political climate TC is increasingly seen to be significant only as a stage of transition towards the now more ideologically acceptable bilingual approach which involves the use of natural sign language. It is the bilingual approach which we shall now consider.

Chapter 4
The Bilingual Approach

Bilingualism is a relatively new idea in deaf education and one which has attracted a lot of recent attention and interest. Bilingualism can be seen as a reaction against both oral-only and TC approaches. Bilingualists share with advocates of TC the view that an auditory-oral approach fails to meet the communication and linguistic needs of children with substantial hearing losses. But bilingualists are equally critical of TC and accept the criticisms of both the theory and the practice of TC outlined above. Hence, bilingualists agree with the view that combining speech with a contrived system of signs does not bring verbal language to deaf children. Furthermore, they believe that TC in the form of simcom does not directly offer a language in sign. TC is perceived to be speech centred and speech does not, so it is argued, serve the developing deaf child's communication and language needs. The trend towards use of TC during the 1970s in the USA and during the 1980s in the UK is perceived by bilingualists as good only insofar as sign became formally recognised as having a role to play in the education of deaf children. The introduction of TC has been successful in persuading many former oralists to become more 'flexible' in their attitude towards sign and prepared to acknowledge that an oral-only approach does not meet the needs of at least some deaf children.

Bilingualists firmly believe, however, that TC involves the wrong sort of signing. The signs of SE or SSE are artificially contrived and do not stand in their own right as a 'proper' language. A frequently used analogy is that putting signs from a natural sign language, such as BSL or ASL, and reconstructing them to follow an English format is like taking the words of Russian and putting them in English word order and adding the grammatical features of English. In neither case do you achieve a 'true' language.

A 'real' language does exist, say bilingualists, which can meet the linguistic needs of deaf children and that is the natural sign language which has evolved over the years through use by deaf people, for example ASL or BSL. Since most profoundly deaf people, it is claimed, communicate with one another in sign (Bench, 1992), it is suggested that sign is the natural language of the deaf: their 'biologically preferred' mode (Charrow, 1975). Young deaf children, left to communicate among themselves, have been observed 'naturally' to develop a gestural code of communication (Heider and Heider, 1941; Tervoort, 1961). That sign languages have not only survived but have thrived, despite the efforts of oral educators, is an indication of their strength and legitimacy as the natural languages of the deaf (Bouvet, 1990). Thus, fundamental to the bilingual approach is that the first language of all deaf children should be the sign language which belongs to the Deaf community of the country concerned*.

Bilingualists consider access to sign language, as a first language, is the birthright of all deaf children. However, as the nomenclature suggests, there is support for *bi*lingualism and acknowledgement of the deaf child's need for verbal language. Literacy is an important goal for bilingualists because they accept that without the ability to read and write an individual is handicapped in a society where so much knowledge and information is contained in written form: there can be no equal opportunities without literacy and every deaf child has the right to be literate (Swift Parrino, 1990). However, for bilingualists the route to verbal language is different from that advocated by supporters of oralism or TC. There appears to be universal advocacy of learning verbal language as a *second* language. A verbal language, such as English, should be taught only when the first language, sign language, has become established in the developing deaf child. With both oralism and TC the aim is that English should be acquired as a *first* language. (TC, in theory, offers verbal language in a signed form but there is no explicit aim to offer sign language as a language in its own right.)

The Case for Bilingualism

A New Ideology

There is a strong ideological and moral component to the bilingualist argument. It is argued that in the first place deaf individuals are not deviant hearing people but are members of a linguistic minority who have a special identity which is different from, but certainly not inferior to, that of hearing people. Only a deaf person knows what it is like to

---

*There is no universal sign language – sign languages, like spoken languages, vary from country to country and even region to region within countries. Whilst there are certain structural similarities between sign languages from different places, most of the 'content' signs are different (Kyle and Woll, 1985).

be deaf and, therefore, it is wrong for hearing people to set themselves up as 'experts' on deafness. It is even more wrong for hearing people to see deafness as an unhealthy condition which needs to be cured. Deafness is only a handicap insofar as hearing people, the dominant group, make it a handicap by trying to force the deaf individual to conform to hearing–speaking norms. This has been referred to as the 'normalisation' conspiracy (Merrill, 1981). Merrill (1976) elsewhere claims:

> The total subjection of a deaf child to a means of communication which he cannot understand in a school setting is not only unprofessional and usually ineffective, but it could well be viewed as a violation of the rights of another human being (p. 2).

Deaf people need to be accepted in society and respected for what they are, that is, as members of a cultural minority not as flawed versions of hearing people. According to Bouvet (1990), hearing teachers of the deaf are amongst the worst culprits in the normalisation conspiracy: most hearing teachers, she contends, want deaf children to conform to hearing norms because of their own lack of familiarity with the world of the Deaf. She claims that, through fear and prejudice, hearing teachers do not like Deaf adults and do not want their deaf pupils to become Deaf adults. They thereby attempt to deny the existence of deafness. Bouvet, and indeed many other writers, argues that deaf children must be allowed to be Deaf and they need to be socialised so that they have the opportunity to acquire a Deaf identity (Ladd, 1981; Lucas, 1989; Sacks, 1989; Bouvet, 1990). This line of thinking leads to the imperative that deaf children should have access to other deaf children and adults and that every step possible should be taken to ensure that they acquire their own language.

Through sign language, so it is argued, the handicap of deafness is eliminated. Through sign language Deaf people 'can understand everything, express everything', (Mottez, 1990). The deaf individual will 'always come out a loser' if he or she has to follow hearing rules (Mottez, 1990). A greater recognition of sign language and a greater willingness to offer information in sign language is what is needed to prevent the unjustified and unnecessary discrimination against the Deaf.

The rhetoric of depathologisation of deafness is echoed in and supported by current notions about handicap and disability. The 'social oppression' theory of disability proposes that it is not so much the individual's loss of function which causes problems of access to a 'normal' way of life but the social and physical environment. The environment, designed for and by the able-bodied, sighted and hearing, etc. restricts activities and opportunities for certain members of society and thereby creates handicap (Oliver, 1990). Many barriers could be lifted if policy-makers so wished or if minority members of society had greater influence on policy: for example, a wheelchair user is only restricted in cinema-going by the lack of ramps or lifts in cinemas and spaces for wheelchairs in the auditorium. In similar vein, a deaf individual is only a handicapped television viewer because of lack of subtitles or sign language interpretation of most TV programmes. The current ideology rejects the medical model of disability and the notion of disability as a defect. It supports the 'normalisation' of disability in terms of the idea that it is normal to be different.

People with disabilities, armed with a new ideology which puts the onus of many of the difficulties they face on the shoulders of society itself, have become more assertive and 'political'. Self-advocacy groups have emerged recently in Britain which seek to change paternalistic attitudes towards themselves as dependent members of society deserving 'pity' and 'charity' but not meriting equal status or equal rights (Sutherland, 1981; Williams, 1982; Oliver, 1990). Equal access to education, employment, income, housing, leisure facilities is what is required and there is the growing feeling that the only way to get access to socially desired goals is for people with disabilities to form themselves into pressure groups and act on their own behalf.

Deaf people, during the 1970s and 1980s in both the UK and the USA, have become increasingly aware of themselves as a minority group and political activism has grown. Not only is there rejection of the medical model of disability but also a denial that Deafness is a disability. That sign language was legitimized as a real language and not just a sequence of mimetic gestures did much, according to many commentators, to develop a new sense of pride in being Deaf (Woodward, 1982; Ladd, 1988; Padden and Humphries, 1988; Sacks, 1989). Referring to recent developments in the USA, Sacks (1989), reports:

> an increasing sense that people could be profoundly different, yet all be valuable and equal to one another; an increasing sense, specifically, that the deaf were a 'people', and not merely a number of isolated, abnormal, disabled individuals (p.148).

Moreover, Deaf people in America were starting to think of themselves not only as a cultural group but as a group with *power*. Perhaps one of the most spectacular manifestations of Deaf Pride and Deaf Power was the 'revolution' at Gallaudet College, Washington, USA, 1988. When the deaf students learned that a hearing President was to be appointed, despite the existence of deaf applicants for the post, the students 'took to the streets', demonstrated with banners and placards and thereby hit the headlines not just in the US media but all over the world (Lucas, 1989; Sacks, 1989). The outcome of the protest was that the newly selected President resigned and a President who was *deaf* was appointed. The Gallaudet event represents a notable example of 'self determination' and has no doubt contributed to the development of 'Deaf Awareness and Deaf Power' in many parts of the world.

Sacks (1989), believes that the level of political awareness amongst deaf people in the UK 'may not yet match that in the United States'. Nonetheless, there is, he acknowledges, 'a large and vital deaf community' which forms a nucleus of Deaf life. It is certainly the case that Deaf communities in some areas of the UK have sought to influence policy with respect to the education of deaf children and there are examples of their success: the adoption of a bilingual policy in deaf education in Leeds Education Authority was influenced by the opinions of an active and vigorous local Deaf community (Pickersgill, 1991).

A Language Appropriate to Ability

The idea of allowing the deaf child to acquire sign language as a first language is supported, so bilingualists claim, on sound theoretical grounds. Academic linguists who have examined and analysed sign language have concluded that sign language is a 'proper' language with its own structure and morphological features. Sign language has the same linguistic status as any verbal language (Stokoe, 1960; Bellugi and Klima, 1972; Brennan, Colville and Lawson, 1980). Natural sign not only serves deaf children as a means of communication between other sign language users but can support intellectual development and the acquisition of knowledge and ideas in the same way that spoken language serves hearing people. It is, therefore, a folly, say bilingualists, to create an artificial sign system, such as SE or SSE, when a bona fide sign language already exists. It is not only a folly but, say most supporters of bilingualism, a moral crime to attempt to force young deaf children to do something they cannot do, that is, learn spoken language as a first language. Deaf children need a 'voice' which is adapted to their abilities and, so the argument goes, the only way a deaf child can acquire the feedback to support language acquisition is through their unimpaired senses of sight and movement. So, only sign language can restore for the deaf child the natural conditions for language acquisition. Drawn into the visual language of sign the deaf child becomes free of handicap (Bouvet, 1990).

British Sign Language

Since the acquisition of sign language is so central to the bilingual argument it will be helpful to examine the main features of British Sign Language.

Linguists who have described and analysed natural sign languages have demonstrated that sign language is as complex and comprehensive a means of communication as any verbal language. BSL, for example, like any other language, is a code for conveying information which is governed by rules. Unlike verbal languages, however, sign language is not conveyed through an acoustic medium but through the articulation of gestures formed by the hands. Manual signs are augmented or modified by facial expression and body posture. Stokoe (1960), the American linguist who was the first modern linguist to analyse sign language, reports that just as spoken language is made up of linguistically significant elements called phonemes, so sign language is made up of elements which he calls *cheremes*. There are three categories of chereme: place or location markers, the position of the hands in relation to the body; configurational markers, the shapes of the hands; and action markers, the type and direction of the movement of the hands. The relationships between the elements are spatial rather than sequential: the cheremes are arranged simultaneously to create a sign. Action markers mean nothing without configuration and location and all three elements are necessary for the formation of a sign.

Signs may share, say, handshape and movement but differ in location. So, for example, the BSL signs for CAR and DRIVE have the same handshape and movement but are different in their location, with DRIVE occupying more space than CAR (Kyle and Woll, 1985). Handshape and location may be the same but a different movement can differentiate two distinct signs: for example, both THINK and THOUGHTFUL are made with right index finger in the area of the upper part of the head but THINK is made with contact of finger and head and THOUGHTFUL is made with a circular motion (Smith, 1990). In sign language many sign bases or roots can be manipulated in space or by movement to create meanings which are semantically related but are not identical in meaning. So, in BSL, the root sign LOOK can become STARE or SCRUTINISE or LOOK FREQUENTLY AT according to the manner of movement or use of space. Handshapes or configurations can vary a great deal and one or both hands may be used in BSL. The sign for GOOD and the sign for BAD share a location and movement but differ in handshape: GOOD is made with a thumb up and BAD with a little finger up (Kyle and Woll, 1985).

Facial expression is integral to signing and different expressions can change the meaning of a base sign. In BSL, BALL and BALLOON share the base sign but BALL becomes BALLOON by puffing out the cheeks (Kyle and Woll, 1985). The sign for BAD can be changed to mean TERRIBLE through a change of facial expression and a more tense body posture (Kyle and Woll, 1985). Facial expression and body posture in many instances change meaning in a similar way to intonation in spoken English (Miles, 1988).

Through different combinations of handshapes, movements and locations, facial expressions and body postures, an infinite number of signs, broadly equivalent to words, can be articulated in BSL, as in other sign languages.

A distinctive feature of all sign languages is that they contain a proportion of signs which are iconic. Signs which are iconic bear some sort of resemblance to the object or concept referent. For example, in BSL, the sign for CAT is made by a two-handed gestural indication of 'whiskers'. The sign for HOUSE involves making an outline with the hands of a roof and side walls of a house. Some iconic signs are more like metaphors, for example, the sign MAN in BSL is made by gesturing a beard. When people are signing at normal speed the signs may be made quickly enough for the iconicity to be hard to detect. Many signs are quite arbitrary, that is, the symbol has no relationship to the referent. For example, in BSL the sign for EASY involves the index finger extended and crooked, touching the cheek repeatedly (Kyle and Woll, 1985). The sign WHEN involves fingers extended and spread, pointing up, with fingertips flickering at the cheek. Some signs are called esoteric or semi-iconic because the transparency of the sign becomes apparent only when the meaning or derivation is explained. For example, all the BSL signs for BOY involve movement across or down the chin as a way of indicating the smoothness of a boy's chin.

A common device in sign language for creating lexical items is to compound existing signs. Hence, in BSL, the sign for THINK and the sign for TRUE are made simultaneously to indicate BELIEVE (Smith, 1990). Another example is the simultaneous production of THINK and COMPLICATED to indicate CONFUSED (Smith, 1990).

Sign languages, such as BSL, have a distinctive morphology and structure. There is a tendency in sign language to deal with morphology spatially rather than sequentially. Hence, for example, in spoken languages 'I create', 'I created' are dealt with by sequential affixation to the base word. In sign, the distinction is made by the simultaneous production of the base sign and a marker representing the past tense. Similarly 'Create', 'Creation' and 'Creatively' are differentiated in sign by small differences in movement with the base sign CREATE. Singularity and plurality in English are commonly marked by the absence or presence of suffix 's'. Sign language, however, uses repetition or reduplication for plural marking (Kyle and Woll, 1985).

The structure of sign language is different from, say, English, as indeed many verbal languages differ from each other in terms of their syntax. In English (unlike, say, Latin) word order is very important and a basic Subject-Verb-Object (SVO) pattern is common. BSL, in common with other natural sign languages, is ordered, generally following a Topic-Comment principle (Miles, 1988). The main topic of an utterance is signed first and then elaborated on with some following comment. Deuchar (1984) offers some examples:

CLEAN ALL   =   I cleaned everything

TEN P PUT IN   =   I put in ten p.

One further feature of a natural sign language, such as BSL, which needs emphasising is that information can be conveyed as quickly and efficiently through sign as with spoken language. Bellugi and Fischer (1972) have observed, in relation to ASL, that it takes twice as long to articulate a sign as to say an English word. However, they also observe that the overall rate of information transmission of ASL is roughly the same as for spoken English. Bellugi and Fischer (1972) investigated the time taken by bilingual individuals to read a story aloud and later to sign the story using ASL. In both modes, approximately the same amount of time was required for the telling and no significant information was lost in the ASL version. This was so despite the finding that the ASL version contained 272 signs and the spoken version 405 words. This is a ratio of sign to word of 1:1.48. This apparent anomaly is caused by the capacity of sign language to produce morphological and semantic features *simultaneously*, a feature already noted above. Signs, in natural sign language such as ASL or BSL are, thereby, more 'weighty' than are words in English. (The feature of simultaneity is not found in signed forms of English and, therefore, the signs of SE *do* take longer to produce than the spoken version).

This rather scant description of BSL does not describe a natural sign language in anything like its full complexity. However, the aim has been to demonstrate that, whilst the structure of BSL and ways of conveying meaning are different from those of all verbal languages, essentially BSL *has* structure. There *are* rules and, according to the analysts of sign language, *any* concept or idea can be expressed as efficiently through sign language as through any verbal language. For a fuller description of BSL, aided by helpful graphic or photographic illustrations, readers are recommended to read the following:

British Deaf Association. (1992) *Dictionary of British Sign Language/ English*, London: Faber & Faber

Deuchar, M. (1984) *British Sign Language*. London: Routledge and Kegan Paul

Kyle, J.G. and Woll, B. (1985) *Sign Language. The Study of Deaf People and Their Language*, Cambridge: Cambridge University Press

Miles, D. (1988) *British Sign Language: A Beginner's Guide*, London: BBC Books

Smith, C. (1990) *Signs Make Sense*, London: Souvenir Press.

The Acquisition of Sign Language

Evidence which is used to support the idea that sign language should be the first language of deaf children, and that it is the natural language of deaf children, comes from observations of young children who are reared in a sign language environment.

There have been a number of studies of children of deaf signing parents which have plotted the children's linguistic progress during the early stages of language acquisition. Almost all of the accumulating evidence suggests that deaf children exposed to sign language in the early years acquire language following a pattern that is very similar to the pattern of spoken language acquisition in hearing children. Petitto (1988), for example, observing deaf infants developing in signing homes, has reported that sign babbling occurs which is similar to the sound babbling of hearing infants: the infants 'play' with a variety of gestures and hand movements, in an analogous way to the 'playing with sounds' of hearing infants, at about the same stage of life.

Schlesinger and Meadow (1972), in the USA, studied a deaf infant of deaf signing parents over a period of 8–22 months. The authors reported that at the age of 10 months the infant was making approximations of recognisable signs; at 12 months she produced distinctly recognisable signs; at 17 months there were two-sign combinations; at just over 19 months the child had a sign lexicon of 142 signs. The authors noted that not only is the pattern of language acquisition strikingly similar to the pattern of language acquisition of hearing children but that the child's vocabulary was greater at the end of the study period than an average hearing child of the same age.

Bellugi and Klima (1972), also in the USA, studied a slightly older deaf child, from a signing home from the age of 2;10 to 3;6. The authors reported that two-sign utterances extended to three- or more sign utterances over the period of study in much the same way as spoken utterances extend with hearing children. They also found examples of sign over-generalisation which functioned exactly as the word over-extensions commonly observed in hearing children. So, for example, the deaf child would use the sign for DOG to refer to any four-legged animal.

There are several other examples of similarity between the sign acquisition of deaf children and the word acquisition of hearing children: Caselli (1983), researching in Italy, reported that two-sign combinations occur in deaf children at the same age as two-word combinations are found in hearing children; Folven, Bonvillian and Orlansky, (1984–5) provide evidence that when deaf children first use signs they do so to refer to objects, individuals and events within the immediate context in the same way that hearing children initially use words; Petitto (1987), studying a deaf child acquiring ASL, noted pronoun reversals, e.g. *I/you* confusions similar to those found in hearing children. This latter finding is perhaps surprising given that the signs themselves, unlike the equivalent words, are so transparent, consisting of gestures pointing at the relevant person. It suggests that the signs are indeed operating as true linguistic symbols.

If these findings about sign acquisition can be generalised then it seems to be the case that the mechanisms of the brain underlying the acquisition of sign language are the same as those underlying the acquisition of spoken language. Sacks (1989) explains the phenomenon in terms of Chomsky's (1968) concept of 'deep structure' of grammar. Chomsky proposed that general linguistic competence is genetically determined and species-specific to humans. So, every human being is born with innate mechanisms, latent in the nervous system, for the acquisition of language. These mechanisms, the precise nature of which is unknown, remain latent until kindled by language experience. Almost without exception, young children are exposed to a language and readily acquire whatever language surrounds them. The particular form of grammar, what Chomsky calls 'surface' grammmar, whether it be English, Chinese or French, is determined by the experience of the individual. The underlying facility for acquiring language, however, is the same for all individuals and according to Sacks (1989):

> the grammatical potential is present, even explosively present, in every child's brain, and ... will leap out and actualize itself given the least opportunity (p. 46).

Given that the deaf child has the same language potential as any other child then the only reason deaf children fail to acquire language is that they are given insufficient language experience. This is, sadly, according to Sacks, too often the case when deaf children are exposed to spoken language. However, the language potential does 'leap out' when the deaf child experiences sign language. The surface structure of sign is different: it involves different kinds of signals and different sensory mechanisms. With sign it is space which is 'grammaticized' but the deep structure of sign language and spoken language is, says Sacks, identical. That deaf children can realise their linguistic potential through natural sign language is further confirmed by evidence we have already considered, namely, that when deaf children are exposed to manually coded English, they, (in the US context), 'tend to innovate ASL-like forms with little or no input in that language' (Gee and Goodhart, 1988). It would seem that our 'deep structure' supports the development of natural sign but does not support the development of an artificially contrived language such as Signed English. Hence the claim that 'Sign is closer to the language of the mind' (Sacks, 1989).

The reports based on studies of children acquiring sign language as a first language are used to support the idea that it is through sign language, and only through sign language, that deaf children can find their 'voice' and can acquire language in the normal way.

Becoming Bilingual

The idea that verbal language, such as English, can best be learned through sign language draws support from the ideas of modern bilingual 'theorists', such as Cummins (1984). Cummins notes that in many Western countries children, whose mother-tongue is different from the majority language, take up a disproportionate number of places in special education for children with learning disabilities. Cummins emphasises, however, that acquiring two languages does not of itself lead to any learning disability or cognitive deficit. The problem is that schools fail to respect the childrens' first language and fail to exploit and develop it for 'conceptual and analytic thought'. Cummins believes that if children come to an English-speaking school with a different language as their first language (L1), then there is a strong case for consolidating and strengthening L1 by using L1 as an educational medium. This means, particularly in the early stages of education, offering information and knowledge through L1 or at least *not* forcing the child to produce English (L2), of which he or she has only a superficial knowledge. L2, must, of course, be taught since this is the principal medium of academic development but crucial to Cummins' argument, is that it is *not* necessary to become orally proficient in L2, (in our case, English), in order to be *literate* in L2.

Based on his research in North America Cummins suggests that literacy and academic skills in L2 can best be achieved through making use of the child's well established knowledge of L1. Instruction in reading and writing will be effective, he argues, only if it is 'embedded in a meaningful communicative context', that is, if it is related to the child's previous experience. Attempting to teach literacy through L2, of which the child has only a surface oral competence, is not so effective and can cause delays in the acquisition of literacy which in turn causes learning difficulties. According to Cummins (1984):

> we can predict that students instructed through a minority language for all or part of the school day will perform in majority language academic skills as well or better than equivalent students instructed entirely through the majority language (p. 150).

The important theoretical point is that underlying L1 is a basic linguistic competence which can be applied to the learning of all languages. A first language, if properly established, facilitates the development of the structures and vocabulary of another language. Learning L2 through L1 merely respects the principle of what Cummins terms: 'the common underlying proficiency'.

According to this line of reasoning if deaf children have natural sign language as their first language then underlying their sign language is a linguistic proficiency which can be used to acquire English or L2.

Cummins (1984), commenting in a North American context, believes that deaf children have been discriminated against and disadvantaged educationally by a lack of respect for and acknowledgement of their first language:

> there are strikingly sociological, linguistic and educational similarities between the situation of deaf children and that of other ethnic minority children who experience academic failure ... their language and culture have been denigrated and suppressed at school and their school failure blamed on linguistic and intellectual deficits ... The reasons for incorporating ASL into the instructional programme offered hearing-impaired children are essentially the same as is the case in other minority groups experiencing school failure ... (p. 214).

Bilingualists, in the context of deaf education, reason that sign language is the *only* language which can give young deaf children an underlying language proficiency by the time they reach school age (Johnson, Liddell and Erting, 1989). Deaf children should, therefore, be enabled to acquire sign language in the early years. The school attended by the deaf child, whether a special school or mainstream school, should respect the linguistic knowledge of deaf children and accord their language a proper status. This can be achieved in British schools by, first of all, including BSL in the curriculum (Pickersgill, 1990b) and, secondly, by acknowledging deaf children's language knowledge which means that much of the instruction, at least in the early stages of education, should be through the medium of BSL. Only through natural sign language will the deaf child have a fair chance of access to the whole curriculum (Johnson, Liddell and Erting, 1989). The use of BSL in education, it is claimed, is the only way of not denigrating the child's previous experience and of not undermining his self-respect. Finally, say bilingualists, the school must accept BSL as the essential foundation to the learning of English for academic purposes:

> children can begin the process of learning to read and write from a rich language base in BSL (Pickersgill, 1990b, p. 7).

Bilingualists in the UK believe that through the acquisition of BSL the deaf child has a language for communication, a language for learning and a language for developing English. They argue that no other communication approach can achieve these goals; no other communication approach respects the special abilities and the special identity of the deaf child.

What is Involved in a Bilingual Approach?

Strategies for the Acquisition of Sign Language: the Early Years

Observations of young deaf children, whose parents are deaf and use sign language in the home as the predominant means of communication, inform bilingualists about suitable strategies for sign acquisition. Since signed communication is in a visual modality differences have been noted in the pattern of interaction between the deaf signing parent and deaf child and speaking parents of hearing children (Woll and Kyle, 1989). In the first few months of the deaf infant's life the baby is much preoccupied with the touch, smell and sight of the care-giver and at this stage deaf mothers tend to vocalise more than they sign (Woll and Kyle, 1989). It is when the infant sits up independently and pays attention to aspects of the wider environment that the signing parent starts to communicate in sign. The signing care-giver must gain the deaf infant's visual attention to give information through sign yet at the same time relate the information to the object, or focus of attention, in the environment.

There is, of course, a potential problem of divided focus of attention, which does not feature when parents talk with hearing children, since hearing children can simultaneously attend to objects and events with their eyes and to the message about them with their ears. However, it would seem that signing care-givers can adopt a variety of strategies to overcome the problem of divided attention. Care-givers can manoeuvre themselves into the visual field of the infant and produce a high proportion of signs within the child's focus (Harris et al., 1989). Care-givers can wait for the deaf child to look at them and then produce signs appropriate to the situation (Mills and Coerts, 1990). It is possible to get the child first to attend to the care-giver's face by gently tapping the child, or moving his or her face, then sign what is to be referred to while pointing the (care-giver's) arm in the direction of the object (Woll and Kyle, 1989). A care-giver can point to an object, or picture of an object, checking that the child's gaze is directed towards the object or picture and then redirect the child to the adult and provide a sign for that object (Woll and Kyle, 1989). Another strategy observed is to sign on the deaf infant's body (Maestas and Moores 1980) and to manipulate the child's hands into the shape of signs and guide its movements (Bouvet, 1990). Ensuring that the deaf child is seated comfortably and is supported means that the adult can face the child and at the same time look at pictures or play with toys. In this situation an adult can offer signs without being physically separated from the child (Mills and Coerts, 1990).

According to Gallaway and Woll (1994), deaf mothers are highly successful in making sign communication visible to their young children and the potentially difficult attentional problem does not actually materialise for a child learning to sign in a signing home.

However, we know that the majority of deaf children are born to hearing parents who do not sign. The very big issue that must be addressed, by those proposing that sign language should be the first language of all deaf children, is whether the conditions which are present in the homes of deaf signing parents can be replicated in the homes of hearing parents or, indeed, anywhere else. This problem is not treated lightly by bilingualists but, generally, they share an optimistic belief that there are ways around the problem. Many parents, they claim, if given appropriate support, encouragement and training, can achieve sufficient competence in sign to be able to communicate with their young deaf child in a way that is mutually enjoyable and satisfying.

In Sweden, for example, lavish provision of full-time and part-time courses in sign language is available to all parents of deaf children. Great success in parents' ability to sign is reported (Davies, 1991). It is suggested also that hearing parents can receive invaluable support from deaf signing adults both in the home and in a signing environment such as the local deaf club (Johnson, Liddell and Erting, 1989; Bouvet, 1990; Hansen, 1991; Pickersgill, 1991). Given the importance of a deaf child acquiring sign in the early years bilingualists unanimously believe that deaf adults should be employed to support the learning of sign by parents, so as to provide a model of effective adult–child interaction in sign and to offer the deaf child sign language input.

Bouvet (1990), a French educator, suggests that once parents see through sign that their deaf child really can communicate they begin to form a much more positive view of their child. Parents cease to view their child as incomplete, or deviant, and look upon him or her as uniquely able to 'talk with the hands'. Seeing their deaf child develop sign language is, according to Bouvet, the best way to help parents accept their child's deafness. Furthermore, when hearing parents realise that their child can communicate through sign they become well motivated to acquire and use sign themselves. Parents need only to know a few signs to get a sign response from their child and the pleasure derived from this provides a good spur to learn more signs. Essentially, hearing parents need to be sensitive to the visuality of their child and with this orientation and awareness it is claimed that they can become as adept as deaf parents in visual interaction (Sacks, 1989).

It is recognised that it is not easy for a hearing adult to become a competent and fluent user of natural sign language. For some hearing parents a way into natural sign may be to learn first what for them is the easier form of sign, Signed English, Signed French, Signed Danish, etc. (Bouvet, 1990). According to Sacks (1989), because of the deaf child's natural tendency to 'nativise' towards natural sign-like forms, it does not really matter if parents in the home use a pidgin or rudimentary form of signed verbal language: the children will add appropriate linguistic structures.

However, it is held to be important for deaf children from hearing homes to have contact with fluent signers – deaf signing children and deaf signing adults – and steps should be taken to provide this experience. Johnson, Liddell and Erting (1989), for example, believe that early experience of the signing of deaf adults is crucial both to language and social development:

> The acquisition of a natural sign language should begin as early as possible in order to take advantage of critical period effects ... The best models for natural sign acquisition, the development of a social identity, and the enhancement of self-esteem for deaf children are deaf signers who use the language proficiently (p. 16).

Johnson, Liddell and Erting (1989), recommend that from as early an age as possible deaf children should spend a considerable part of the day in specialised nursery facilities where they can become immersed in the signing of the deaf adults employed there.

The idea of introducing deaf adults into the lives of young deaf children, for the purpose of providing sign language input, is endorsed in Sweden, where there is approximately a decade of experience of attempts to provide bilingual education for deaf children. O'Rourke (1990), reports on the basis of a visit to Sweden:

> In Sweden, they did something very simple. They realised that hearing parents are not going to be effective role models from which a deaf child can learn sign language. Therefore, as soon as a child is identified as being deaf, the hearing parents are paired with a deaf couple, who act as deaf role models for the child – sort of foster parents. The deaf children continue to live with their own parents, while at the same time learning a lot from their deaf foster parents (p. 12).

Davies (1991), from the USA, having visited both Denmark and Sweden, confirms that in both countries it is universally accepted that hearing parents cannot be linguistic models for their deaf children. However, she reports immense enthusiasm for learning 'deaf' sign language on the part of hearing parents and very positive attitudes to the use of sign in the home.

Learning Through Sign: The School Years

Given that the deaf child receives appropriate sign language experience in the early years then it is assumed that by the time the deaf child reaches school age he or she has achieved the linguistic competence necessary to have access to the normal school curriculum (Johnson, Liddell and Erting, 1989). This is in distinct contrast, bilingual supporters emphasise, to deaf children exposed to an oral-only or a TC approach who typically start school with a significant language delay. Following the bilingual principle of using the child's first language for educational purposes the curriculum should be offered in sign language. Those who offer curricular content to the children must be fluent signers. For this to be achieved it is extremely important, so the argument goes, to make considerably more use of deaf signing adults in formal education than is currently the case (Pickersgill, 1990a). It is advocated that there should be wider opportunities for deaf young people to train as teachers of the deaf, and also far greater use of deaf people as communicators\interpreters\instructors in the classroom both in special and mainstream schools (Pickersgill, 1991). Very few teachers of the deaf in Britain are accomplished in BSL and this is seen, by those advocating a bilingual approach, as an enormous failing on the part of most teacher-training institutions. However, even if the situation were 'improved', in this respect, bilingualists still emphasise that a contribution must be made by deaf signing adults. Just as those learning French need to go to France, to *really* learn the language, so there is a need for deaf children to be exposed to 'native' users of sign language (Lucas, 1989). In the British context, offering education through the medium of BSL not only ensures full access to the curriculum but also strengthens the development of the child's BSL language abilities.

Presenting the curriculum to deaf children in BSL is seen as an equal opportunities issue: if deaf children are to have the same access to education as hearing children then BSL has to be the primary language of instruction. Again, following the principles of Cummins outlined earlier, it is BSL, as the L1 of deaf children, which should be used to enable the child to acquire L2, that is, English. So, according to Johnson, Liddell and Erting (1989):

> English will be taught as a second language and methods of English instruction will take advantage of the first language competence the children already have (p. 16).

Amongst bilingualists there now seems to be almost universal approval of approaching English via the written rather than the spoken form (Johnson, Liddell and Erting, 1989; Bouvet, 1990; Hansen, 1990; Davies, 1991). The reason for not approaching verbal language through speech is the belief that essentially deaf people perceive language in a visual and not in an auditory way. The process of learning to read can be undertaken entirely through visual means using the written text and using sign language as a vehicle for explaining written language.

Several accounts have been offered about techniques for approaching written text through sign language (Akamatsu and Armour, 1987; Evans, 1987; Strong, Woodward and Burdett, 1987; Christensen, 1989). Essentially, it is suggested that sign language be used as a meta-language so that the symbol system of sign is used to understand the symbol system of English. It is important, therefore, that as part of this process deaf children are enabled to come to an understanding of the linguistic principles of sign language, of the way it is structured and formed. Through an understanding of BSL as a language it is then possible, so it is argued, to understand the principles of organisation and formation of symbols of another language such as English (Akamatsu and Armour, 1987). Learning the visual form of English through a visual language means approaching the written symbols in a more holistic way than would be the case when hearing children learn to read (Ewoldt, 1985; Hansen, 1990). It is not, so it is argued, appropriate to break down the written words into their acoustic elements where children can have no perception of those elements. Whole words and whole phrases should be explored, and examined, primarily for their meaning and the concepts they embody.

So, it is recommended by bilingualists that verbal language should be approached in a visual rather than an auditory way and it is claimed that deaf children will achieve literacy in this way (Strong, Woodward and Burdett, 1987; Christensen, 1989; Johnson, Liddell and Erting, 1989; Bouvet, 1990; Stewart, 1990). The question of the role of speech in the education of deaf children remains. Is verbal language in the *spoken* form considered to be a goal of bilingualism? The answer here is not very clear and there appear to be differing views. Hansen (1990), reporting from Denmark, where there are a few years of experience of the use of a bilingual approach in the education of deaf children, suggests abandoning the goal of spoken language:

> Although in recent years deaf people have defined themselves as a linguistic minority with Danish Sign Language (DSL) as their primary language and Danish as their second language, no deaf person actually masters both languages fluently ... So however idealistic we might be when setting up the goals for a bilingual education of deaf children, we will – in order to respect the identity of any deaf person as a person having a hearing loss – also have to modify our expectations and teaching methods when it comes to their learning of a second language, which involves a sense they do not have. So our definition of a bilingual deaf adult must exclude the notion of being able to speak a language (p. 1).

Johnson, Liddell and Erting (1989), on the other hand, believe that speech can be taught, but only after competence in verbal language has been established through literacy:

> Understanding and producing speech are skills to be developed not as a means of acquisition, but as a result of acquisition, after competence in the language has been established through literacy (p. 17).

These authors do not preclude 'the use of early auditory stimulation and vocal practice' but emphasise:

> that a primary focus on hearing and speech should not be allowed to hinder normal age-level acquisition of language or knowledge' (p. 18).

Though they do not specify the strategies needed, these authors recommend that:

> The development of speech-related skills must be accomplished through a program that has available a variety of approaches, each designed for a specific combination of etiology and severity of hearing loss (p. 18).

The bilingual programme at the Royal School for the Deaf, Derby, England, explicitly aims to give 'equal status to both British Sign Language and English' (Royal School for the Deaf, 1989). As with other bilingual programmes described, sign language is the main language for 'communication, teaching, discussion, etc.' and reading is encouraged as a way of helping the children learn the rules of English. For 40 minutes a day there is an oral English session (without signs) in order to facilitate the children's oral communication skills. Fluent and intelligible spoken language is not, however, the prime goal and it is assumed that 'some of the children will never have good speech, or make use of their hearing aids'. The programme is currently being studied by a research team from the Open University to see if the bilingual approach 'really improves the children's education'. It will be of great interest to see if this British 'experiment' succeeds in bringing both English and sign language to deaf children.

The use of signs and speech together, as in sim-com, is clearly forbidden by bilingualists but it would seem that the development of spoken language in parallel with the development of sign language is permissible so long as sign language remains the primary means of instruction (Bouvet, 1990). It is made clear by Johnson, Liddell and Erting (1989), however, that sign language and spoken language should not be used together in any one context:

> Sign language and spoken language are not the same and must be kept separate both in use and in the curriculum (p. 16).

The picture we have, of what is involved in a bilingual education for deaf children, is one where nearly all instruction is through natural sign and that deaf children are offered, through sign language, the same 'broad and balanced' curriculum that is available to all schoolchildren. For the children to be immersed in a signing educational environment it is important, particularly from the point of view of their language development, that many more fluent deaf signers are involved in the education of deaf children. The approach to verbal language is through the written form and the aim is that literacy will be achieved through mastery of, and an understanding of, the linguistic principles of BSL. Oracy *per se* does not seem to be a major goal, if a goal at all. Lack of oracy is not, in any case, perceived to be a serious problem: the acceptance of deaf people in society is not to depend on their ability to speak. The aim of education of the deaf is to provide language and access to knowledge and this, so the argument goes, can be well achieved without speech. Deaf people need to be respected for what they are, not for what they cannot be. Bilingualists strongly support the principle embodied in a comment made by the Commission on Education of the Deaf in the USA (1988) that: 'there is nothing wrong with being deaf'.

An Evaluation of the Bilingual Approach

One problem with attempting to evaluate the efficacy of a bilingual approach is that we do not, in the UK, nor in the USA or Canada, have sufficient experience of use of the approach to know whether or not deaf young people emerge from it as fluent signers and as literate, knowledgable and well informed people. A consideration of the premises, arguments and assumptions of bilingualism, however, raises many questions which we can examine. Policy statements on the approach, such as: 'Unlocking the Curriculum' by Johnson, Liddell and Erting (1989), have provoked considerable discussion and controversy (O'Rourke, 1990). Before examining the different views on the principles of bilingualism, however, it may be useful to summarise the bilingual case. The main elements of the argument seem to be these:

1. Deaf people should be recognised not as handicapped individuals but as a cultural and linguistic minority group with rights of access to education, employment, etc. equal to those of other members of society.
2. Natural sign languages have the same linguistic status as verbal languages.
3. Deaf children have the right to acquire their own 'indigenous' language, sign language, as a first language.
4. Given appropriate experience, deaf children acquire sign language at the same rate and in a manner that is very similar to the way hearing children acquire spoken language.
5. Hearing parents, if offered appropriate support, can communicate comfortably through sign with their young deaf child.
6. Deaf signing adults have an important role to play in helping hearing parents acquire sign communication and in developing sign language in deaf children.
7. Deaf children should be educated through the medium of sign language as only then will they have full access to the normal school curriculum.
8. Deaf children can become literate, that is, acquire verbal language

in the written form through the language base of natural sign language.

9. It is morally wrong to impose on deaf children a language they cannot apprehend, that is, spoken language.
10. The linguistic potential of the deaf child can be realised only through being enabled to acquire sign language as a first language.

We need now to consider the different views and critical comment on bilingualism as it is currently defined. Some components of the bilingual argument are not disputed, or at least not disputed much, and these will be considered first.

The Deaf as a Cultural Minority

On the issue of the rights of the deaf community as a linguistic minority, no-one would deny that those deaf people who wish to form themselves into a group should have the right to do so. Deaf individuals, like anyone else, should be free to associate with whoever they choose. Furthermore, it is certainly the case that many adults, who have been profoundly deaf since birth, can communicate more freely and fluently through sign rather than spoken language. This makes the idea of joining a group of similarly situated people, with whom communication, and thereby companionship is easy, a very attractive proposition. The psychological and social benefits of belonging to a community are undeniable. The image of the deaf individual, who becomes isolated because of an inability to communicate through speech, is unacceptable to all.

Deaf groups, of course, have the right to perceive themselves as a linguistic and cultural minority, if they so wish, and the right to become politically active in order to support their interests. To ask to be accepted as equal, though linguistically different, members of society is not an unreasonable claim where there is an inability, or a great difficulty, in communicating through spoken language. It could be reasoned that since people with paraplegia are not asked to walk, then deaf people should not be expected to talk. People with paraplegia should have mobility and opportunity through wheelchairs, and wheelchair access, and deaf people, therefore, should have access to communication and information through sign language and sign language interpretation.

That deafness does *not* impose a handicap is more open to question but educators, whatever their favoured communication approach in the education of deaf children, would not, I suggest, deny the deaf individual the right to a special 'Deaf' identity if that is his or her choice. Nor would they deny the right to use sign language as a preferred means of communication. Nor would anyone deny the right of deaf people to join with other deaf people to pursue collectively common interests in gaining access to what is generally available in the wider society and in fighting discrimination and prejudice.

The Linguistic Status of Sign Language

Another aspect of bilingualism which is not generally challenged is the status of natural sign languages, such as BSL or ASL, as legitimate languages. Those advocating an auditory-oral approach or TC generally do not argue that natural sign cannot transmit information and ideas effectively. The most notable exception in this respect is Van Uden (1986). Readers who wish to follow his arguments in detail are advised to read his book: *Sign Languages Used by Deaf People, and Psycholinguistics: A Critical Evaluation*. Essentially, Van Uden argues that sign language, as commonly used by deaf people, is more of a pidgin than a fully-fledged language and does not, therefore, have the same capacity as verbal languages for conveying knowledge, information and ideas. Since the deaf signing community is small there has not been the opportunity for sign to become as well developed or enriched a language as, say, English, which is used by hundreds of millions of people all over the world. Van Uden gives examples of sign communication which he believes demonstrate that signs in use are context-bound and do not stand alone as communication unless that context is very well understood. Meanings are implicit and the iconic nature of all sign languages make it less capable of expressing abstract ideas than verbal languages where the symbols are arbitrary. This viewpoint can be challenged (Bench, 1992) on the grounds that the meaning of much everyday spoken language is tied to the immediate context. Also, that some signs are iconic does not mean that they cannot symbolically convey complex ideas or abstract thought. However, critics of the proposal that natural sign should be the first language of deaf children do not, I believe, rest their case on the grounds that BSL or ASL are not proper languages and they do not, on the whole, challenge the assertions of linguists and others about the linguistic status of sign language.

The Acquisition of Sign Language as a First Language

The evidence used to support the contention that deaf children, exposed to natural sign language in the early years of life acquire sign in a similar way to hearing children acquiring speech is another feature of the bilingual argument which is not currently challenged. However, Harris (1992), reporting some UK research undertaken by Harris et al., (1989), suggests that we need more data, on larger samples of deaf children acquiring sign, before drawing any firm conclusions on this matter.

The investigation of Harris et al,, (1989) involved observations of four profoundly deaf children together with their profoundly deaf mothers. In all cases the children's deafness had been diagnosed before the age of 3 months. In all cases BSL was the main language of the home, and the fathers were deaf. Three of the children were observed in free play with their mothers at intervals between the ages of 7 months to 2 years and one was observed from the age of 15 months to 2 years. The mothers varied in their style of interaction and in the way in which they used sign with their children. However, throughout the period of study, most of the signed utterances of the mothers were single signs; the amount of signed input was considerably less than the amount of speech which is reported for hearing mothers of hearing children and with considerably fewer lexical items. The sign language development of the children was recorded and whilst there were variations between the children all were, for their age, considerably behind what is average in spoken language development of normally hearing children. At the recording at 24 months, one child produced 16 different signs; one, 7 different signs; one, 1 sign and the other produced no signs at all. Although the recording was only for 20 minutes the mothers confirmed, in the case of each child, that this was a fair estimate of the children's signing ability. So, according to this study, even the most linguistically advanced deaf child was delayed in language production when compared to a hearing child developing speech. The language delay of the children and the relatively limited input of the mothers was interpreted by the researchers as being related to the problem for mothers of not being able to coordinate their signing with the focus of attention of the child.

These findings appear to contradict those of other investigations, some of which have been cited above. Harris (1992) did not want to dispute previous claims 'since they appear reasonably convincing'. However, she draws attention to the fact that many of the children previously studied had 'highly educated parents' and that 'relatively little is known about the range of vocabulary development that occurs within the whole population of deaf children born to deaf parents'.

A further problem, not explicitly raised by Harris but which arises from the Harris et al., (1989) study, relates to the assessment of sign language development. Is an account of lexical items a proper measure of sign language acquisition? Do all deaf children achieve competence in sign language via the same route? Can we provide norms of acquisition of sign language by which to judge the level of sign language achieved by any individual deaf child? Do we have a way of deciding when a child has acquired mastery of the syntax of sign? Are there different levels of sign competence achieved by deaf children and young people? At the moment it would seem that we are not in a position to answer these questions.

A problem with evaluating sign language ability is that the available standardised tests of language are based on verbal language assessment. Several writers, for example, Kannapell, (1989); Kyle and Ackerman, (1990); Hansen, (1990), have pointed out that such tests are not generally suitable when applied to sign language attainments and do not take into account the many language features which are peculiar to sign. Hatfield (1982), reviewing research where there has been an attempt to assess ASL, argues that the studies are flawed by inadequate definition of sign language and by inappropriate test techniques.

It would seem that if the claims are to be sustained that full linguistic competence and age-appropriate language acquisition can be achieved by offering natural sign language, there is a pressing need for the development of new tools for the assessment of sign language at different stages of acquisition.

Those who have anxieties and doubts about the bilingual approach may not challenge evidence which suggests that deaf children, *if* given appropriate sign experience, *can* develop sign at a rate similar to the rate achieved by hearing children in acquiring speech. What is of more concern to critics is whether deaf children ordinarily *will* develop sign language which is good enough to support their ability to receive education and to achieve literacy. The study cited by Harris (1992) suggests that creating a facilitating environment for sign language acquisition can be problematic even when the parents are deaf themselves and sign users. There is evidence which indicates that hearing parents attempting to use sign have difficulties in sustaining interaction with their deaf child. Woll (Gallaway and Woll, 1994) in her review of studies of sign language input and sign language acquisition, cites a UK study by Gregory and Barlow (1989) which compares the interaction of nine hearing and seven deaf mothers all of whom were using sign with their deaf infants. They found that the deaf mothers were more successful in establishing patterns of interaction, joint activity and mutual play than were the hearing mothers. The children with deaf mothers attended to their mothers more than the deaf children with hearing mothers; deaf mothers were more attentive to the child's focus of attention than were the hearing mothers. Gregory and Barlow also compared reading activities of a hearing mother\deaf child dyad with a deaf mother\deaf child dyad at 24, 30 and 36 months. They found that the deaf child with the deaf mother participated more actively in the interaction than the deaf child with the hearing mother.

Woll (Gallaway and Woll, 1994) cites a US study by Swisher (1990) which, she suggests, confirms that 'hearing mothers appear not to have access to the strategies employed by deaf mothers'. Swisher investigated hearing mothers using sign systems with their deaf children. She found that the children aged 4–6 years were seeing in their entirety only about two-thirds of their mothers' signed utterances.

The studies of hearing parents signing with their deaf children seem to be showing that there are problems in establishing mutual interaction in sign. Other studies, for example, Bornstein, Saulnier and Hamilton (1980), indicate that hearing parents have difficulties in learning to sign competently. Yet these studies, almost inevitably involve well motivated mothers, keen to learn sign in order to advance their children's language acquisition through sign. The question that arises, then, is: what happens when parents or care-givers are not well motivated to learn sign or do not have the time to put aside for learning sign, or who find sign difficult to grasp and give up learning sign almost from the start? There is evidence from the USA (Weisel, Dromi and Dor, 1990) that positive attitudes towards signing are associated with socio-economic status: the lower the socio-economic status, the less interested parents are in learning sign (SE) to use in the home. If this finding can be generalised, deaf children from lower socio-economic backgrounds are disadvantaged in terms of sign language environment. At the present time, in both the USA and the UK, there is little experience of inviting parents to learn ASL or BSL. It might be speculated, however, that since natural sign is harder for hearing people to learn than Signed English, the pool of parents willing and able to learn ASL or BSL will further reduce.

So, critics of a bilingual approach believe that it is not unreasonable to assume that if there were a universal policy of bilingualism, then many, if not most deaf children, would not, in the early years, for a variety of reasons, receive satisfactory sign language experience in their homes.

Supporters of bilingualism, as we have seen, believe that a possible solution to the problem of ensuring an adequate amount of sign language experience for the young deaf child is to introduce adult deaf signers into the homes of deaf children of hearing parents. This is so that the deaf adults can help parents with their signing and provide some sign input to the child. Parents, observing a deaf adult in interaction with their deaf child, can learn from the strategies used some techniques for interacting in the visual mode. However, there are problems with this 'solution'. Firstly, it has to be established whether or not there are enough adult deaf people willing to spend time or be employed in the homes of deaf children. It is by no means clear that, in a given community, there will be this source of support. Furthermore, in the US context, Markowicz (1990), comments that deaf people can be possessive of their language, for good sociolinguistic reasons, and, therefore, not willing to share ASL with hearing people. Secondly, it is not at all self-evident that adult deaf people, who can sign fluently, will be able to teach signing to hearing people or be suitable people to work with young children. Thirdly, it might be unacceptable to some parents to receive another adult into their homes for the purpose of 'taking over' the communication development of their child.

An alternative option, and one which might make better use of the 'scarce' resource of deaf signing adults, is to take the children out of their homes for much of the day and place them in specialised nursery facilities where they can acquire sign language from deaf adults, other deaf children and\or natural sign-signing teachers. Johnson, Liddell and Erting (1989), who suggest this practice, believe that parents should not be excluded from this provision and, in fact, should be encouraged to participate. However, it is not likely that many parents would or could attend the nursery for any length of time. A policy of removing a deaf child to a specialist all-signing centre may have the desired effect in promoting sign language acquisition, and in supporting the socialisation of the deaf child into the Deaf community, but this does not help the parent communicate with the deaf child. There is a serious danger that the young deaf child will grow apart from his or her hearing family.

Lucas (1989), writing on the sociolinguistic aspects of deafness, offers the accepted 'sociolinguistic reality' that language defines one's identity and group loyalty. If that is the case, then as Johnson (1990) points out, there is likely to be a problem of either the deaf child becoming completely alienated from his or her hearing family or suffering a clash of identities and a sense of divided loyalties, feeling to be both a member of a hearing family and a member of the Deaf community.

The weakening of a deaf child's links with his family may be the price that must be paid if the goals of bilingualism are to be achieved: it may be necessary if deaf children are to be given language through sign and are to be socialised to be 'Deaf', that the primary agents of socialisation must be other deaf children and adults encountered outside the home. But most parents, educators, deaf individuals, would probably agree with Greenberg (1990), that 'the family' is very important for the healthy development of the deaf child both in the early years and throughout his education. The responsibility for the deaf child's psycho-social development cannot, nor should not, he says, be given over to schools. Greenberg emphasises that 'we do not want deaf children rejecting their hearing parents in order to be part of the deaf community'.

There seems to be no easy way of reconciling the 'needs' of deaf children for a supportive home and the 'needs' of deaf children for natural sign language as both a first language and a means of defining their personal identity. The 'rights' of parents also becomes an issue. If, for whatever reason, parents cannot learn natural sign with any degree of fluency, and if they do not wish to 'lose' their child to the Deaf community, have they the right to choose another communication option? Have they the right to 'deprive' their deaf child of his or her 'native' language? The question of who has the right to determine the type of education and communication approach that a deaf child should receive is not problematic for bilingualists alone. However, in view of the insistence of bilingualists on sign as a first language, the issue of 'rights to decide' is one that should be addressed.

Access to the Curriculum through Sign Language

The foregoing discussion casts some doubt on whether the 'ideal' conditions, of deaf children being born into deaf signing families, can be replicated for the overwhelming majority of deaf children who are born to hearing, non-signing parents. There must be uncertainty also on the possibility of realising the bilingual proposal that deaf children should receive the bulk of their education through natural sign language. Woodward et al., (1987), on the basis of an analysis of some data from Gallaudet Research Institute, report, in the USA in 1985, that out of a sample of 609 elementary school teachers not one stated that they used ASL as a primary means of communication in the classroom.

Things may be different now that bilingual ideas have had more time to influence those who educate the deaf. However, the majority of teachers of the deaf currently working in the USA and the UK are 'hearing' and have not received training in ASL or BSL. Teachers who have invested time in becoming competent in Signed English may be resistant to learning a new and very different form of signing. Even when teachers are well motivated to apply a bilingual approach, and keen to learn ASL or BSL, there are still problems. Erting (1988), comparing the interaction of deaf signing children with a deaf adult by use of ASL and a hearing teacher attempting to use ASL, reports a much greater degree of misunderstanding between deaf child and hearing teacher than between deaf child and deaf adult. Trotter (1989), investigated the attitudes of teachers of the deaf towards ASL and also looked at their ability to use ASL. Whilst the teachers were found to have positive attitudes towards ASL, they nonetheless betrayed English-like forms in their signing.

Markowicz and Woodward (1978), based on their observations, in the USA, of deaf people signing with both hearing and other deaf people, report that when deaf and hearing people sign together the signing of both groups is more English-like but when deaf sign with deaf the signing is ASL-like. The authors interpret this observation as meaning that not only do hearing people find it difficult to use ASL but that ASL is an in-group language – *the* in-group language of the culturally Deaf. ASL in the USA, according to Markowicz and Woodward, functions as a device for maintaining an ethnic boundary between Deaf and hearing people. If this is so, then it looks as though natural sign is relatively inaccessible to hearing people and largely in the hands of the Deaf.

These assorted research findings all seem to indicate that hearing people, generally, are not in a good position to learn and use natural sign language. The prospect of the majority of parents and teachers of the deaf becoming fluent in natural sign, therefore, is remote. It would appear that if deaf children are to develop sign language at school, and receive an education in sign, then a great many more deaf signing people will need to be recruited into the classroom, either as teachers or as interpreters\communicators. It remains to be seen whether there is the required reserve pool of adult deaf signing people willing and able to fill these posts.

The problem with offering deaf children an education through the medium of sign need not be perceived as an 'in principle' one but the problems of offering such an education nonetheless suffers from very serious difficulties of feasibility – difficulties, which, it could be argued, cannot be ignored.

The Development of Literacy

If we suppose, however, that natural sign can be the predominant means of communication in the classroom one of its major tasks is to tackle the development of literacy. As we have seen, the theory underpinning the bilingualist idea of learning verbal language in the written form through sign, draws heavily on the theory of learning L2, not by submersion in L2, but by making considerable use of the child's knowledge of L1. Cummins (1984), the main proponent of this approach to the development of bilingualism in children, bases his ideas on data derived from the experience of 'hearing' linguistic minority children developing the majority language in school. There are, however, differences, which may be significant, between the situations of deaf children learning L2 and 'hearing', linguistic minority children, learning L2. In the latter case both L1 and L2 are verbal languages. Developing literacy in L2, using another verbal language as the language base *may* not involve the same processes as the use of a visual–spatial language to develop an auditorily based written language. It may be the case that developing literacy in English from ASL or BSL is more difficult than developing literacy in English from, say, Urdu or Gujerati.

A further point of difference is that, in the case of linguistic minority 'hearing' children, the first language is the one that is used predominantly in the home and as a consequence the children have a good command of the structures of L1 and a sizeable vocabulary in L1. However, this assumption of a well established L1 may not hold for deaf children. As we have seen, the conditions where natural sign is the predominant language of the home are difficult to create. Indeed, Cummins (1984) himself, in the context of ethnic minority families generally, does *not* advise parents to use any language in the home other than their own language:

Educators should *never* advise minority parents to switch to English in the home. This is not only unnecessary in view of the common underlying proficiency principle but it will often have damaging emotional and cognitive effects as a result of the lower quantity and quality of interaction that parents are likely to provide in their weaker language (p. 267).

It would appear to follow that Cummins would not favour 'hearing' parents attempting to communicate with their deaf children in their weaker language, sign language. Given the bilingualist assumption that spoken language is inaccessible to deaf children, critics of bilingualism might conclude that what is being recommended is that most parents of deaf children should not communicate at all with their children.

However, if it can be organised that the deaf child receives some sign language input, whether in the home or out of it, then the deaf child may use sign as a preferred means of communication. But this does not mean that the deaf child, on reaching school age, has achieved mastery of the structures of sign language nor that he or she has a good sized lexicon of ASL\BSL signs. If deaf children at school are still in the relatively early stages of acquiring sign then not only is delivering much of the curriculum in, say, BSL problematic, but the deaf child does not approach learning to read from a 'rich language base of BSL' (Pickersgill, 1990b). Unless the problems associated with offering deaf children an enriched natural sign input in school can be solved the deaf child may still have insufficient 'underlying proficiency' in sign language to develop L2 by the time that they need to in order to make normal educational progress. What is being questioned here is the analogy between the linguistic and educational circumstances of deaf children and 'other ethnic minority children who experience academic failure' (Cummins, 1984). There *are* differences and these differences may be highly significant.

Though research evidence is scant, there has been some small scale research which has looked at the use of natural sign to develop abilities at written English. Akamatsu and Armour (1987) report, on the basis of a study of deaf high school students, that offering instruction about the rules of ASL, and comparing those rules with the rules of English, improved the students' ability to produce and understand written English. The authors judged the intervention to be successful though they warn that it is not likely that many teachers are familiar enough with ASL and its rules to be able to offer that form of instruction.

Another potential problem with developing literacy from the deaf child's sign language, and presumed 'preferred' means of communication, is one of motivation to learn verbal language. Given that sign language has such symbolic importance in defining a Deaf individual's identity, Maxwell (1990) suggests that deaf children and young people, in order to retain their special identity, may want to distance themselves from the hearing and not want to have anything to do with 'hearing' language.

Most of what is written on the topic of the use of natural sign to develop verbal language in the written form describes possible strategies and argues that this is the 'way forward' for developing literacy in deaf children, but the literature does not provide much in the way of evidence of either success or failure. Pickersgill (1990, 1991), for example, argues forcibly for a bilingual approach in the education of deaf children in the UK and offers proposals for implementing a bilingual policy, but cannot, as yet, give us confirmation that the approach is successful in developing genuinely bilingual deaf children because the data are not yet available. Johnson, Liddell and Erting (1989), similarly do not offer evidence from the USA, or from anywhere else, that the bilingual education they describe yields the hoped-for results. Sacks (1989), reports 'widespread and successful use of bilingual education' in Venezuela and Uruguay and describes educational programmes similar to those proposed by Johnson, Liddell and Erting (1989), where deaf children and infants are sent as early as they are diagnosed, to be exposed to deaf signing adults until they are old enough to go to a nursery school. Sacks (1989) asserts that: 'Both of these South American programs have already achieved notable success and hold out great promise for the future', but he supplies no survey evidence of achievements.

Lindahl and Andersson (1990), describe an approach to bilingualism used with deaf children in Sweden and claim that: 'through Sign Language they (deaf pupils) have also gained a better understanding of Swedish and better confidence in using this language'. These authors again furnish us with no evidence based on the standards of Swedish achieved. Hansen (1991), reporting on the experience of bilingual education in Denmark, claims that: 'the reading skills of deaf children have improved tremendously since the bilingual approach was implemented in 1980s'. If this is so, why can we not have some facts and figures to confirm the claim?

Bouvet (1990), in her description of a bilingual class for six deaf children in France, offers some examples of written language which are impressive in terms of the standards of French achieved. However, the examples are taken 'almost exclusively from our youngest student, Agnes, who benefited the earliest from bilingual education'. A report of 'success' in one child only would generally not be regarded as 'evidence' that a particular approach was effective.

The aim of bilingualism is to bring two languages to deaf children. Yet there is no firm research evidence that the model of offering sign language first, and verbal language through the written word second, can deliver two languages to the average deaf child. The bilingual programmes described or advocated vary in minor ways but they share a lack of emphasis on verbal language as a means of education and a lack of emphasis on spoken language in the deaf child's linguistic development. Moores (1992), speaking from the USA, is a firm believer in the value of ASL as an educational tool but he nonetheless doubts whether any approach involving almost exclusive use of ASL can be 'truly' bilingual. Commenting on certain bilingual programmes, in the USA, Moores (1972) observes:

> Frankly, I found it difficult to understand how any program could advertise itself as bilingual-bicultural if it does not allow English in person-to-person communication. It seemed to me that efforts to repress English in one of the programs were punitive and excessive (p. 307).

The emotional attachment to the model of bilingualism displayed above should not preclude anyone thinking about alternative ways of introducing both sign and verbal language, spoken and\or written, to the developing deaf child. Let us consider the oralist view of how deaf children might be enabled to acquire both spoken and sign language.

Fundamental to the oralist argument is that in offering verbal language through spoken language and in developing the deaf child's hearing ability and capacity for speech, the deaf child is being offered something in the early years which cannot be recovered later on: it seems most likely, so the oralist argument goes, that if deaf children have not learnt to use their residual hearing for the discrimination of speech by the time they reach young adulthood then they have probably lost this capacity for ever. Bench (1992) suggests:

> the experience of auditory and other stimuli during certain stages in child, and especially infant, development has profound and lasting effects on later behaviour, especially language behaviour. Should such experiences be denied, the child will experience long-lasting deleterious effects in the acquisition of hearing and listening skills and the development of speech and language (p. 18).

That an oral approach in the early years facilitates speech reception and production, and does not undermine other achievements, is indicated by a study by Parasnis (1983). He compared deaf college students who had deaf parents and were native ASL users with college students who had hearing parents and had learned sign between 6–12 years, on a number of cognitive and language measures. The delayed sign group performed significantly better than the native ASL group on tests of speech perception and speech intelligibility and there was no difference between the groups on cognitive skills or on language abilities (language was presented through spoken, written and sign modes).

It can be argued, therefore, that it *is* possible to learn sign, later on, without any previous experience of signing in childhood. Many orally educated deaf adults have chosen to learn sign language as young adults and some now communicate primarily through sign, (Winston, 1990). It seems to be the case that many Deaf individuals, currently prominent in the Deaf community in Britain, had little or no experience of sign as children. This suggests that becoming bilingual by acquiring oral language first and learning sign language at a later stage is a genuine communication option. Moog (1988), based on her knowledge and research of deaf people in the USA, certainly believes this to be the only proven way to bilingualism for the deaf individual:

> There is no evidence that shows a profoundly deaf child can be taught simultaneously to sign and speak and do both well. There is also no evidence that a child can first become a competent signer and then learn to speak well. However there is evidence that if you become a competent talker, you might later acquire signs if you wanted to be able to use both systems. Everybody that we've ever studied who was competent with both modes, learned to speak first and sign later (p. 1).

It may be true, as Sacks (1989) argues:

> that those who learn Sign late ... never acquire the effortless fluency and flawless grammar of those who learn it from the start ... (p. 83).

But, that so many deaf individuals do learn to sign late and understand the signing of others reasonably effectively suggests that, for most purposes, sign language acquisition is possible in adolescence and adulthood. Kyle and Woll (1985), suggest that if deaf people choose to learn sign at some stage in their lives a very powerful motivation and a strong feeling of identification with the Deaf group, greatly facilitates their being able to acquire sign. Kyle and Woll (1985) argue that it is the absence of social and psychological distance between deaf people which makes the acquisition of sign language relatively easy for them when compared with hearing people learning sign language.

The oralist 'solution', then, is to develop oral language first, teach literacy through oral language and then offer access to sign language afterwards. Oralists, in short, argue that the best route to bilingualism is by facilitating the acquisition of sign language as a *second language*: quite the opposite of what is recommended by 'bilingualists'. Both oralists and advocates of TC might claim that offering verbal language as a first language is the only reliable way of enabling the deaf individual to become bilingual.

Indeed, it has been argued that the rhetoric of 'bilingualism' and 'biculturalism' is a euphemism for one-language (sign language) and one-culture (Deaf culture) (Moores, 1992).

It may be, however, that there are other ways of delivering sign and word. For example, if the goal of oral language is not to be sacrificed, and if fluent signing is to be established at as early a stage as possible, it might be feasible to develop spoken language and sign language in parallel. Cornett (1990) gives some individual examples of deaf children who developed spoken language and natural sign during childhood. In all cases both sign and spoken language were acquired in spontaneous face-to-face interaction. Natural sign was learned from native users of sign and verbal language was learned from hearing people through the medium of speech. Good models of each language, therefore, so Cornett argues, were provided in both languages. The languages were learned independently and there was little mixing of the two codes: signs were used almost exclusively with signing people and speech with hearing people. Cornett claims that this form of bilingualism 'worked' for these deaf children and that the concurrent use of two languages, varying according to social and linguistic context, is a pattern of bilingualism commonly observed with people using two or more verbal languages.

The Moral Argument for Sign as a First Language

The argument for delivering verbal language as the top priority in deaf education, supported equally by oralists and TC advocates, has already been made. There remains, however, a need to answer, or at least discuss, the accusation made by bilingualists of a 'normalisation conspiracy': the allegation that both oralism and TC create handicap by attempting to convert deaf children into something they can never be – hearing–speaking people.

Oralists and TC supporters believe this accusation to be unfair. They fully share with bilingualists the belief that the deaf child has the same facility for language acquisition as a hearing child and that activating this capacity is central to deaf education. They believe, however, that the deaf child's linguistic potential can be realised by presenting verbal language direct, either purely orally or, in the case of TC, with the help of signs. They consider that delivering verbal language as a first language *is* achievable and there is no need, therefore, to involve a different type of language which has little currency in the wider society.

Oralists and advocates of TC do not accept the bilingualist claim that offering verbal language as a first language represents a denial of deafness, a discounting of difference, but, rather, they say it is giving deaf children what they most need, spoken language and literacy. They recognise that there is: 'nothing wrong with being deaf', just as there is nothing wrong with being blind or having short stature. The reasoning followed by oralists and advocates of TC to defend this position is that all humans are different and everyone has limitations and vulnerabilities: what is wanted, they argue, is a society which recognises and fully accepts human differences – a society which does not discriminate unfairly against people because they are different. Oralists and TC adherents reject any accusation of 'disablism' and believe themselves to be just as concerned with 'empowerment' as bilingualists. Thus, those who subscribe to oral or TC approaches argue that the moral arguments are not all on the side of the bilingualists.

Having looked at the case for bilingualism, it would seem that the claims made by bilingualists are based more on what a priori seems to be right, and on 'moral' grounds, rather than on hard research findings on the linguistic and other educational achievements of deaf children. That there is no firm evidence that bilingualism can be attained, however, does not mean that the bilingual approach cannot achieve the intended aims. It may take time to work out effective strategies for developing natural sign in deaf children where sign language is not the language of the home; to develop tools for measuring sign language development and competence in deaf children and deaf young people; and to give deaf children literacy on the basis of sign rather than spoken language. (On the latter point, Ramsey (1990) from the USA, argues that whilst a way has not yet been found to get to verbal language through ASL and printed English, there will nonetheless eventually be a 'deaf solution'.) There are sufficient numbers of people, very determined on ideological grounds that deaf children should be offered sign language as a first language, to make the quest for finding a way of arriving at verbal language through sign a continuing enterprise in the future (O'Rourke et al,1990).

The support for introducing sign as the first language of deaf children is claimed to be based, as we have seen, on strongly held moral principles. Critics can disagree with the current model of bilingualism but cannot, of course, 'prove' that bilingualists are morally wrong. Indeed, in the current ideological climate it is difficult for critics even to continue to argue that deafness *is* a disability and a problem which must be overcome. It appears to be 'politically incorrect' to contest let alone condemn the idea of giving natural sign as a first language to deaf children, given the symbolical meaning sign language has for the Deaf and given the respect claimed by and generally offered to the Deaf as a cultural and social group. The problems for many deaf children in achieving fluency in sign on reaching school age and problems for teachers in delivering the curriculum in sign, and in developing verbal language through sign, are seen as technicalities – practical difficulties which are challenging, but which are *capable* of being overcome. Bilingualists share with Christensen (1989), the view that: 'an educator should attempt to change the world rather than just sit in it'. For bilingualists the argument, that deaf children have the right to acquire *their* language as a first language, the only language in which they are not handicapped, is unassailable, and the moral case for bilingualism rests there.

Chapter 5
Discussion and
Conclusion

What seems to emerge from my exploration of communication options for the deaf is a situation of uncertainty and moral dilemmas. The auditory-oral approach, though more successful in giving oral language to deaf children than in years gone by, still does not guarantee fluent spoken communication for all profoundly deaf children. Total Communication, at least as widely practised, has made little contribution to the overall raising of academic and linguistic standards of deaf children. The bilingual option is relatively untried and untested as currently conceived, but can be questioned on the practical grounds of difficulty of implementation, if on no others. The moral issues of *who* should make fateful decisions on behalf of young deaf children and *what* decisions should be made are weighty to say the very least.

It would seem that LEA Services for Hearing-Impaired Children in the UK, faced with these dilemmas, and aware of a need to appear flexible and offer choice, are increasingly offering more than just one comunication approach. Bloor (1993) recently surveyed provision of communication approaches in all 108 of the LEAs of England. He reports that only six (5.55%) LEAs offered, or made available, an oral-aural approach exclusively and only a further six (5.55%) offered, or made available, TC only. Just over half the Services, 57 (52.77%) offered directly, or made available, an oral-aural *and* a TC approach. Interestingly, 31 (28.70%) Services claimed to offer or make available oral-aural *and* TC and bilingual approaches. The remaining six (5.55%) LEAs offered either a combination of oral-aural *and* bilingual or TC and bilingual approaches. By no means all the provision of signing was confined to the special schools. Bloor confirms the findings of others, that in the UK many units for hearing-impaired children in mainstream schools use some sort of sign approach (Powers, 1990).

Bloor (1993) did not attempt to judge the quality or consistency of use of any of the approaches claimed to be on offer. Nor did he examine what Service providers understood by his definitions of 'oral-aural', 'TC' and 'bilingual'. The survey did not reveal whether there was an open choice between the options for, say, all the profoundly deaf children, or whether particular approaches were predesignated for particular groups of deaf children. Traditionally in the UK the use of signs as part of a communication approach has been reserved for deaf children with additional disabilities or for deaf children who appear not to be making progress with spoken communication and it is likely that the thinking behind this tradition persists.

If it is the case, however, that more communication options are available for more deaf children, this trend in policy towards offering a variety of educational options will be pleasing to many. It could be argued that if each approach were available in every area for all profoundly deaf children then the problem of 'which approach?' is solved. Parents could be presented with the alternatives and appraised of the implications of the different approaches so that they could then make an informed decision on behalf of their deaf child. Professionals, on the basis of their expert knowledge and experience, could contribute to the decision-making process and help ensure that each deaf child received an education according to his or her individual needs. However, I believe that the problem of 'which approach?' is very far from solved in this way and that a number of complex issues and practical difficulties remain.

In the first place, given the small size of the profoundly deaf child population (about 1:2000), it is unlikely that all LEAs will be able to offer all the communication options themselves. Many LEAs would probably only be able to make available, for example, bilingualism, a 'highly demanding of resources option', by sending children away from their homes for residential placement out of the Authority. (They may, of course, pay 'lip-service' to offering this option, but that is another matter.) In the second place, many, if not most, LEA Services for Hearing-Impaired Children offer types of educational placement and communication options which reflect the past and current views of those responsible for that provision. This means that even when different communication options are available, educational provision within an LEA area is geared to preconceived notions of the 'needs' of deaf children. Parents, as newcomers to the scene, are likely to be directed towards what is available and believed to be suitable rather than what is theoretically possible. Individual parents are not, generally speaking, in a position to influence, let alone determine, the types of educational option that are going to be accessible in their geographical area.

Thirdly, even if it is accepted that it is the parents of the deaf child who should make the decisions, parents must have information before they can take a reasoned decision. Helping parents understand the issues and the implications of different options is a formidably difficult task, since, as I hope I have demonstrated, the issues are not simple nor clear-cut. The problem for parents in being able to make a rational choice is exacerbated by the need to make decisions at a time when most parents are having difficulties, emotionally, in coming to terms with their child's deafness. Moreover, the commonly accepted idea that all that professionals have to do is offer information impartially about the different communication aproaches and then leave it to the parents to make up their minds is, in my view, disingenuous. It is true that not all educators align themselves exclusively with one communication approach, but there are many who do and who are committed to an auditory-oral or TC or bilingual approach at least for most of the profoundly deaf children they come across. Where there is commitment to a particular approach then it is difficult, even for professionals, not to allow the information they present to parents to reflect their preferences or bias. And parents confronting deafness in a child, probably for the first time in their lives, actively seek advice and positive guidance. Generally speaking, they want more than to be left alone with a large quantity of information which is difficult to unravel and assimilate.

A further very serious question to be addressed is that even if all three broad communication options could be properly implemented and made available to all profoundly deaf children, and even if all the information about these options and their implications could be presented in a genuinely impartial way, should it be parents, and parents alone, who have the final say in determining the education and communication approach offered to deaf children? Professionals who work with deaf children are committed to doing what they believe to be in the best interests of each individual deaf child. It is deaf children who are their clients, deaf children whom they are paid to serve, not parents. Most professional educators believe, rightly or wrongly, that their specialised knowledge and expertise *should* influence the judgement made about the education offered to a particular deaf child. Where there is a conflict of opinion between professional and parent, who has the right to the final decision?

A 'solution' to the problem of 'who decides?' frequently put forward is that decisions about communication approach should be based on 'individual needs'. The reasoning used here is that all deaf children are different and they, therefore, have different needs. No single approach, so it is argued, will be suitable for all deaf children: some deaf children, because of their individual characteristics, need a pure auditory-oral approach; some need speech supported by signs; some need to acquire natural sign as a first language; some need different approaches at different stages of their development. It is up to parents and professionals working together to determine the deaf child's characteristics and ascertain needs, and it is then up to the educational service to provide for those needs. However, I believe this line of reasoning to be faulty. Indisputably, no two deaf children are alike in every respect. However, it is surely the case that it is adults, professionals in particular, who *define* deaf children's needs. Children do not have their 'needs' stamped on their foreheads. That this is so is evidenced by looking at the variety of practices, past and present, which have been used to give language to deaf children. Deaf children have not intrinsically changed over the years, but ideas about 'good practice' certainly have (Bates, 1985).

So if, for example, a deaf child is currently judged to be 'visual' rather than 'oral' in his or her attitudes, this may relate to intrinsic features in the child, or it may relate to features of the deaf child's environment. Whatever the 'real' reason, it is likely to be professionals who not only make the judgement about the child's characteristics in the first place, but also determine whether those characteristics prescribe one approach rather than another. Frequently, amongst professionals there is disagreement about both kinds of matter: a lack of consensus about the nature of the child's attributes and a lack of consensus about the communication approach which is most suitable given the existence of those attributes. Individual educators may perhaps agree that there are deaf children who need signing support for their communication development and deaf children who can develop verbal language without the aid of signs. However, there is undoubtedly disagreement concerning which children fall into which category. Decisions about selection of communication approach are, I suggest, to a significant extent determined by the ideas of educators rather than by intrinsic, unalterable features of the child. I would argue that advocates of all three approaches that have been considered, are 'fighting the same ground', that is, by and large they are arguing about the needs and interests of the 'same' deaf children according to their distinct viewpoints.

The question of ownership of the right to make decisions on behalf of young deaf children, who are not in a position to choose for themselves, is central to the current 'communication' debate and I will try to elucidate the issues here. To take first the bilingual position: fundamental to bilingualism is the belief that all deaf children have an inalienable right to 'their own language' as a first language. This means that deaf children must be offered sign language as a matter of priority in the early years. This position is particularly strongly supported by Deaf adult members of the Deaf community who perceive the situation as a 'human rights issue' and claim to speak on behalf of 'Deaf people' themselves. The 'right' of young deaf children to sign language as their own language is not, of course, determined by the child himself. The Deaf community, therefore, strongly challenge the rights of parents and educators to decide any approach other than the 'sign language as a first language' option. The point was made forcefully by Clive Mason at the 3rd National LASER Conference:

> Clive Mason was angry at the plight of deaf children in households where parents refused to sign. This, he said, was child abuse as surely as if these parents had locked their child up in an attic and left it to rot. He felt that deaf children should be removed from homes where the parents abused their children in this way. (British Deaf News, 1990, p. 6).

However, leaving the question of parents' rights aside, I contest this position on the grounds that it is not the case that all adults deaf from birth belong to the Deaf community and choose to identify primarily, or even at all, with the cultural and social world of the Deaf. According to Kyle and Woll (1985):

> Not all deaf people wish to be associated with the deaf population and many of them choose to work and socialise with hearing people ... 29% of profoundly deaf people (in our study) rarely go to the deaf social club ... (p. 7, p. 11).

So, it has to be asked whether it is axiomatic that *some* adults who are deaf have the right to dictate educational provision for *all* deaf children? It seems that the Deaf who demand sign language as a first language are little concerned with the parallel or even later development of spoken language. I do not deny that there may be possibilities in the future for the development of a form of bilingualism which *does* allow for and genuinely seeks the parallel development of spoken language along with sign language. What I am challenging is the *current* idea put forward by members of the Deaf community and some educators that sign language should be the first and only language in the early years and that spoken language is either an unimportant or unachievable goal. It would appear that some Deaf people are *de facto* claiming *all* deaf children as future members of the Deaf community. It would seem that they are insisting that all deaf children, regardless of their potential ability to develop the use of their residual hearing for the development of oral communication, become Deaf, that is, become socialised into the Deaf community and Deaf culture. There is, of course, nothing wrong with identifying primarily with the culturally Deaf, but deaf children who have the bilingual route selected for them, will have little or no choice but to be Deaf as adults. I am suggesting, here, that it is not safe to assume that had the deaf individual been given the choice, he or she would always choose the Deaf route to their future development as a social being. If there is any uncertainty or doubt about the answer to this question, then the right of some adults who are deaf to make such fateful decisions on behalf of all deaf children must be seriously questioned.

If it is accepted that deaf adults who choose to be culturally Deaf do not necessarily have the right to determine the communication approach offered to young deaf children, then what of the claim of oralists or TC advocates, who are generally speaking hearing educators, to know what is best for deaf children and prescribe a form of education which does not involve natural sign language? Oralists in particular are regularly accused of imposing hearing—speaking norms on those who cannot hear and are thus deemed to be guilty of 'cultural oppression' (Ladd, 1991).

Oralists would claim that their status as non-deaf people is irrelevant when it comes to making decisions about deaf children's education. The overriding concern for oralists as professionals and educators is that deaf children be given every opportunity to make maximum use of their residual hearing in order to understand and produce speech. If this opportunity is denied a profoundly deaf child in the early years then deaf children have probably lost for ever the possibility of learning to listen and learning to express themselves through spoken language. Oralists would further argue that even if a minority of deaf children could not succeed in developing fluent oral communication, the majority, who in their view can succeed, should not be denied the opportunity to do so. The argument that we should not try to make deaf individuals talk just as we should not try to make people with paraplegia walk is valid only if it is *impossible* for deaf children to talk. Oralists deny the impossibility of the goal of speech for profoundly deaf children. (Indeed, it might be speculated that if a way can be found to regenerate the nerves of the spinal cord and thus enable people with paraplegia to walk, albeit imperfectly, then many, probably most, will choose to do so.)

If, as oralists believe, the majority of deaf children *can* develop their hearing capacity well enough to be competent spoken language users, then *no-one*, whether a Deaf adult or a parent, has the right to deny deaf children that opportunity. So oralists, if they are true to their position, are equally prescriptive about the rights of deaf children and on the communication approach that should be pursued.

Oralists and advocates of TC may well be hearing people and would acknowledge that they cannot really 'know' what it is like to be deaf. But they, and indeed many deaf people, *do* know of the immense social consequences of not being able to communicate with the majority of members of the society in which they live. Those who are born profoundly deaf from birth represent a very tiny proportion of the population. Difficult though it is for an educator who has normal hearing to make statements on the topic of the social rights of deaf people, it could, nonetheless, be argued that to be able to interact easily *only* within the small world of the Deaf is a restriction of rights. Human rights, as generally understood, mean being allowed access to socially desirable goals and being able to participate in the wider society. Participation in the mainstream of society does not deny allegiance to a minority group. In the UK, there are many who have strong cultural ties within a minority group and who use a minority language when interacting within that group. But the overwhelming majority of minority group members believe it important to be able to engage, socially and economically, with the rest of society and in the British context that means they appreciate the need to speak English.

The developing awareness of the Deaf in the UK, as a minority group, has undoubted significance to the development of the Deaf as a political pressure group. It is likely that in the future, as is the case in North America, more rights will be secured for sign language users in the UK, such as the greater availability of sign language interpretation. However, although there are interconnections between Deaf groups up and down the country, the Deaf Group as a whole forms rather a scattered 'community'. As an exclusive sign language using group which is very small and relatively fragmented, it is extremely unlikely that the Deaf will gain genuine 'equality' and 'equality of opportunity' in a hearing—speaking world. It is likely that to be economically, politically and socially successful, the Deaf must be able to communicate with the majority members of society in the language of that majority. It must be questioned, therefore, whether an individual's full realisation as a member of a democratic society can be achieved solely through membership of the Deaf group.

At an individual level, given the relatively small size of the Deaf population in any town or even city, it could be argued that the Deaf world is rather a restricted one with too little opportunity to associate with a variety of fellow human beings. It is one thing to have a strong sense of Deaf identity of which one can be proud, but is it desirable for an individual to be obliged to focus so strongly on Deafness as a defining feature? Is there enough to 'being Deaf' to sustain an individual as a fulfilled human and social being? It may seem impertinent and indeed improper for a hearing person to ask such questions, but I share with oralists the belief that respect for the rights of Deaf people should not preclude us from questioning whether a deaf individual might not feel resentful if, as a consequence of his or her education, he or she could communicate comfortably only through sign language and was prepared more or less exclusively for the social world of the Deaf.

So, oralists and advocates of TC challenge the bilingual option, which currently places so little emphasis on the development of a widely shared means of communication, on the grounds that it reduces the life-chances of the deaf individual. The auditory-oral option in particular might be seen to impose a difficult communication regime on the young deaf child but if this is so it is only in order to enlarge the future life-chances of the deaf individual by enabling significant participation in the mainstream of society without precluding involvement in the Deaf community.

The TC option shares with oralism the goal of achieving fluent communication in the majority language and has the worthy objective of 'easing the way' to verbal language for the young deaf child by employing a signed version of verbal language. Unfortunately TC has not, up to now, been markedly successful in achieving the objective of promoting language development for deaf children *overall* through a form of Signed English. This is not to say that some form of combination of signs and speech cannot be used to good effect where *full* mastery of language is not the primary goal: in the case of some deaf children it may be appropriate to offer limited but 'functional communication' rather than the full structure of language. Furthermore, whilst subscribing to the oralist position in broad terms, I would challenge oralists who believe that signs can have no role at all in the development of language and in the education of the deaf child. It may be the case, as we have seen, that in the very early days of communication development it is helpful and constructive to use gestures and signs to facilitate the deaf infant's progress towards vocal communication (Robinshaw, 1992). The crucial issue here is at what stage should signs be 'dropped' so that they do not interfere with the deaf child's development of the use of residual hearing. This is an area which is not properly understood and which merits further research.

With respect to the use of signs in the education of deaf children and young people, it is important to distinguish between the use of an approach for language acquisition and the use of an approach for conveying information. Given that at the present time many profoundly deaf individuals, often as adolescents or young adults, have acquired some facility with signing (either Signed English or natural sign language) then it must certainly be constructive to consider whether or not, in some educational contexts, sign language might be used to advantage. For example, it may be the case that although orally competent, a deaf young person, at the later stages of school education or in Further or Higher Education, could receive lecture-style teaching more easily in sign than through the lecturer's speech. This is not to say, however, that the provision of more sign language interpreters at the more advanced stages of education is likely to be a panacea for all deaf students in all contexts. The technical information and advanced knowledge of a lecture, with its associated specialist vocabulary, may be difficult or impossible for sign language interpreters to translate. For some lectures, it may be more sensible to employ the services of a student note-taker. Discussion in a tutorial group may be more difficult to follow via a sign language interpreter than by following the speakers with the help of a well located radio hearing aid. Generally, however, and particularly at the later stages of education, all educators, whatever their communication 'persuasion', should be flexible enough to recognise that there are contexts which may require different communication modes.

It is possible that in the future ways can be found for incorporating signs within an educational context to expand and promote the language competence of deaf children and young people. However, an examination of the TC practice of combining signs and speech and a consideration of the achievements of TC educated children over the past two decades offers little encouragement to persist with that particular way of using sign to promote language acquisition.

In conclusion, having considered the arguments and in the light of current evidence, and the knowledge and experience that we have, I believe that the current critique of TC is justified but also that there are in principle and in practice problems with the bilingual approach. I believe that the use of an auditory-oral approach with young deaf children comes closest to safeguarding the future interests of the deaf individual because of my view that the vast majority of even profoundly deaf children *can* achieve standards of spoken communication which will support significant participation in the hearing world and which can support the acquisition of the secondary language of reading and writing. I believe, therefore, that it is the moral duty of educators to facilitate spoken language. It is only by offering the young deaf child the prospect of talking that the developing deaf individual can be offered the real option of deciding whether or not to take on a predominantly 'Deaf' social identity, or a predominantly 'hearing' identity or to participate equally in both 'Deaf' and 'hearing' worlds.

References

Aitchison, J. (1989) *The Articulate Mammal*. London: Unwin

Allen, T. (1986) Patterns of academic achievement among hearing-impaired students: 1974 and 1983. In Schildroth, A. and Karchmer, M. (eds) *Deaf Children in America*. San Diego: College-Hill Press

Altman, E. (1988) *Talk with me! Giving the Gift of Language and Emotional Health to the Hearing-Impaired Child*. Washington, DC: A.G. Bell Association

Andrews, E. (1988) Conversation. *Journal of the British Association of Teachers of the Deaf*, 12, 2, 29–32

Andrews, E. (1988) The relationship between natural auralism and the maternal reflective way of working. *Journal of the British Association of Teachers of the Deaf*, 12, 3, 49–56

Arnold, P. (1978) The deaf child's written English — Can we measure its quality? *Journal of the British Association of Teachers of the Deaf*, 2, 6, 196–200

Akamatsu, C. and Armour, V. (1987) Developing written literacy in deaf children through analyzing sign language. *American Annals of the Deaf*, 132, 46–51

Babbidge, H. (1965) A report to the Secretary of Health, Education and Welfare by his Advisory Committee on the education of the deaf. *Education of the Deaf*, Washington, DC: US Government Printing Office, 0-765-119

Baker, C. (1978) How does 'sim-com' fit into a bilingual approach to education? In Caccamise, F. and Hicks, D. (eds) *American Sign Language in a Bilingual Context: Proceedings of the Second National Symposium on Sign Language Research and Teaching*, Silver Spring, MD: National Association of the Deaf.

Bamford, J. and Saunders, E. (1991) *Hearing Impairment, Auditory Perception and Language Disability*, London: Whurr (second edition)

Bates, A. (1985) Changes in the approach to encouraging language development in hearing-impaired children. *Journal of the British Association of Teachers of the Deaf*, 9, 6, 140–144

BATOD National Executive Committee (1981) Audiological definitions and forms of recording audiometric information. *Journal of the British Association of Teachers of the Deaf*, 5, 3, 83–87

Beard, R. (1990) *Developing Reading* 3–13, London: Hodder & Stoughton.

Bellugi, U. and Fischer, S. (1972) A comparison of sign language and spoken language. *Cognition*, 173–200

Bellugi, U. and Klima, E. (1972) The roots of language in the sign talk of the deaf. *Psychology Today* 6, 61–76

Bench, R.J. (1992) *Communication Skills in Hearing-Impaired Children*. London: Whurr

Bickerton, D. (1981) *The Roots of Language*. Ann Arbor: Karoma

Bishop, J., Gregory, S. and Sheldon, L. (1991) School and beyond. In Taylor, G. and Bishop, J. (eds) *Being Deaf: The Experience of Deafness*, London: Open University

Bloor, D. (1993) A survey of communication approaches used in pre-school/primary provision for deaf children in England. Unpublished MSc. dissertation, Centre for Audiology, Education of the Deaf and Speech Pathology, University of Manchester

Bornstein, H. (1974) Signed English: a manual approach to English language development. *Journal of Speech and Hearing Disorders* 39, 330–343

Bornstein, H. (ed.) (1990) *Manual Communication: Implications for Education*. Washington, DC: Gallaudet University Press

Bornstein, H. and Saulnier, K. (1981) Signed English: a brief follow-up to the first evaluation. *American Annals of the Deaf* 126, 69–72

Bornstein, H., Saulnier, K. and Hamilton, L. (1980) Signed English: a first evaluation. *American Annals of the Deaf* 125, 467–481

Bouse, C. (1987) Impact of a cochlear implant on a teenager's quality of life: a parent's perspective. *Hearing Journal* September, 24–29

Bouvet, D. (1990) *The Path to Language: Bi-lingual Education for Deaf Children*. Clevedon: Multi-lingual Matters

Brasel, K. and Quigley, S. (1977) The influence of certain language and communication environments in early childhood on the development of language in deaf individuals. *Journal of Speech and Hearing Research* 20, 95–107

Brennan, M., Colville, M. and Lawson, L. (1980) *Words in Hand: A Structural Analysis of the Signs of British Sign Language*. Edinburgh: Moray House Publications

Briggs, L. (1991) A polytechnic with a difference. In Taylor, G. and Bishop, J. *Being Deaf: the Experience of Deafness*. London: Open University

British Deaf Association (1985) *Raise the Standard*. Carlisle: British Deaf Association

British Deaf Association (1990) Bilingualism – teaching English as a second language to deaf children. *British Deaf News* January 1990

British Deaf Association (1992) *Dictionary of British Sign Language/English*. London: Faber & Faber

Byrne, D. (1986) Recent advances in acoustic hearing aids. *Volta Review* 85, 5, 31–43

Caleffe-Scheuck, N. (1990) *Auditory-Verbal Training Program Handbook*. Englewood, CO: The Listen Foundation

Caselli, M. (1983) Communication to language: deaf children's and hearing children's development compared. *Sign Language Studies* 39, 113–144

Charrow, V. (1975) A psycholinguistic analysis of 'deaf education'. *Sign Language Studies* 7, 139–150

Child, D. (1991) A survey of communication approaches used in schools for the deaf in the UK. *Journal of the British Association of Teachers of the Deaf* 15, 1, 20–24

Chomsky, N. (1968) *Language and Mind*. New York: Harcourt, Brace and World

Christensen, K. (1989) ASL/ESL: a bilingual approach to education of children who are deaf. *Teaching English to Deaf and Second-Language Students* 7, 2, 9–14

Clark, M. (1978) Preparation of deaf children for hearing society. *Journal of the*

British Association of Teachers of the Deaf 2, 5, 146–154

Clark, M. (1989) *Language Through Living for Hearing-Impaired Children*. London: Hodder & Stoughton

Clark, M.M. (1976) *Young Fluent Readers: What Can They Teach Us?* London: Heinemann Educational

Cole, E. (1992) *Listening and Talking: A Guide to Promoting Spoken Language in Young Hearing-Impaired Children*. Washington, DC: A.G. Bell Association

Commission on Education of the Deaf (1988) *Toward Equality*. A report to the President and the Congress of the United States. Washington, DC: US Government Printing Office

Connor, L. (1986) Oralism in perspective. In Luterman, D. (ed.) *Deafness in Perspective*. London: Taylor & Francis

Conrad, R. (1979) *The Deaf Schoolchild*. London: Harper and Row

Cornett, O. (1990) Bilingual competence in sign language and spoken/written language. Rochester, NY: International Congress on the Education of the Deaf

Corson, H. (1973) Comparing deaf children of oral parents and deaf parents using manual communication with deaf children of hearing parents on academic, social and communicative functioning. Unpublished doctoral dissertation, University of Cincinatti

Crul, T., Hoekstra, C. and Suykerbuyk, R. (1990) *The effect of early hearing-aid fitting on deaf infants' vocalizations*. Rochester, NY: International Congress on Education of the Deaf.

Cummins, J. (1984) *Bilingualism and Special Education: Issues in Assessment and Pedagogy*. Clevedon: Multilingual Matters

Cunningham, J. (1990) Parents' evaluations of the effects of the 2M/house cochlear implant on children. *Ear and Hearing* 11, 375–381

Curtiss, S. (1977) *Genie: A Psycholinguistic Study of a Modern-Day 'Wild Child'*. New York: Academic Press

DES (1968) The Education of Deaf Children: the Possible Place of Finger Spelling and Signing. (The Lewis Report). London: HMSO

Dale, D. (1984) *Individualised Integration*. London: Hodder & Stoughton

Davies, S. (1991) The transition toward bilingual education of deaf children in Sweden and Denmark: perspectives on language. *Sign Language Studies* 71, 169–195

Davis, A., Haggard, M., Saucho, J., Marshall, D., Hughes, E. and Wood, S. (1988) Standardised Paediatric Audiology Records. IHR Internal Report Series A. No. 6

Denton, D.M. (1976) The philosophy of Total Communication. Supplement to *British Deaf News*, August 1976, Carlisle: British Deaf Association

Deuchar, M. (1983) Is British Sign Language an SVO language? In Kyle, J. and Woll, B. (eds) *Language in Sign: An International Perspective on Sign Language*. London: Croom Helm

Deuchar, M. (1984) *British Sign Language*. London: Routledge and Kegan Paul

Eagney, P. (1987) ASL? English? Which? Comparing comprehension. *American Annals of the Deaf* 132, 272–275

Erting, C. (1988) Acquiring linguistic and social identity: interactions of deaf children with a hearing teacher and a deaf adult. In Strong, M. (ed.) *Language, Learning and Deafness*. Cambridge: Cambridge University Press

Evans, D. and Falk, L. (1986) *Learning to be Deaf*. Amsterdam: Mouton de Gruyter

Evans, L. (1982) *Total Communication: Structure and Strategy*. Washington, DC: Gallaudet University Press

Evans, L. (1987) Reading through sign: the application of theory into practice. In

Kyle, J. (ed.) *Sign and School*. Clevedon: Multilingual Matters

Evans, L. (1989) Some effects of total communication as perceived by parents of deaf children. *Journal of the British Association of Teachers of the Deaf* 12, 5, 142–146

Ewing, I. and Ewing, A. (1961) *New Opportunities for Deaf Children*. London: University of London Press

Ewoldt, C. (1985) A descriptive study of the developing literacy of young hearing-impaired children. *Volta Review* 87, 109–126

Folven, R., Bonvillian, J. and Orlansky, M. (1984/5) Communication gestures and early sign language acquisition. *First Language* 5, 129–144

Freeman, R.D., Carbin, C.F. and Boese, R.J. (1981) *Can't Your Child Hear? A Guide for Those Who Care about Deaf Children*. Baltimore: University Park Press

Fry, D. (1977) *Homo Loquens*. Cambridge: Cambridge University Press

Gallaway, C. and Woll, B. (1994) Interaction and childhood deafness. In Gallaway, C. and Richards, B. (eds) *Input and Interaction in Language Acquisition*. Cambridge: Cambridge University Press

Garretson, M. (1976) Total Communication. *Volta Review* 78, 4, 88–95

Gaustad, M. (1986) Longitudinal effects of manual English instruction on deaf children's morphological skills. *Applied Psycholinguistics* 7, 101–127

Gee, J. and Goodhart, W. (1988) American Sign Language and the human biological capacity for language. In Strong, M. (ed.) *Language Learning and Deafness*, Cambridge: Cambridge University Press

Geers, A., Moog, J. and Schick, B. (1984) Acquisition of spoken and signed English by profoundly deaf children. *Journal of Speech and Hearing Disorders* 49, 378–388.

Geers, A. and Moog, J. (1987). Predicting spoken language acquisition of profoundly hearing-impaired children. *Journal of Speech and Hearing Disorders*, 52, 84–94

Geers, A. and Moog, J. (1989) Factors predictive of the development of literacy in profoundly hearing-impaired adolescents. *Volta Review* 91, 2, 69–86

Geers, A. and Tobey, E. (1992) Effects of cochlear implants and tactile aids on the development of speech production skills in children with profound hearing impairment. *Volta Review* 94, 5, 135–163

Goetzinger, C.P. (1978) The psychology of hearing impairment. In Katz, J. (ed.) *Handbook of Clinical Audiology* London: Williams and Wilkins

Greenberg, M. (1990) Psychosocial development and physical/mental health. Rochester, NY: International Congress on Education of the Deaf

Gregory, S. and Barlow, S. (1989) Interactions between deaf babies and their deaf and hearing mothers. In Woll, B. (ed.) *Language Development and Sign Language* Monograph 1, International Sign Linguistics Association

Gregory, S., Mogford, K. and Bishop, J. (1979). Mother's speech to young hearing-impaired children. *Journal of the British Association of Teachers of the Deaf* 3, 42–45

Grove, C. and Rodda, M. (1984) Receptive communication skills of hearing-impaired students: a comparison of four methods of communication. *American Annals of the Deaf* 129, 378–385

Gustason, G. (1990) Signing exact English: educational tool or social problem? Rochester, NY: International Congress on Education of the Deaf

Hansen, B. (1990) *Trends in the Progress Towards Bilingual Education for Deaf Children in Denmark*. Copenhagen: The Centre of Total Communication

Hansen, B. (1991) *The Development Towards Acceptance of Sign Language in*

Denmark. Copenhagen: The Centre of Total Communication

Harris, M. (1992) *Language Experience and Early Language Development: From Input to Uptake*. Hove: Lawrence Erlbaum

Harris, M., Clibbens, J., Chasin, J. and Tibbitts, R. (1989) The social context of early sign language development. *First Language* 9, 81–97

Harrison, D. (1980) Natural oralism – a description. *Journal of the British Association of Teachers of the Deaf* 4, July Magazine

Harrison, D. (1993) Promoting the educational and personal development of deaf children in an integrated setting. *Journal of the British Association of Teachers of the Deaf* 17, 2, 29–35

Harrison, D., Simpson, P. and Stuart, A. (1991) The development of written language in a population of hearing-impaired children. *Journal of the British Association of Teachers of the Deaf* 15, 3, 76–85

Hatfield, N. (1982) Sign language assessment. In Sims, D., Walker, G. and Whitehead, R. (eds) *Deafness and Communication: Assessment and Training*. Baltimore, MD: Williams and Wilkins

Heider, F. and Heider, G. (1941) Studies in the psychology of the deaf. *Psychological Monographs* 53, 1–56

Hostler, M. (1987) Hearing aid policy with babies and young children. *Journal of the British Association of Teachers of the Deaf* 11, 1, 8–14

House, W. (1976) Cochlear implants. *Annals of Otology, Rhinology and Laryngology*. (Supplement 27) 85, 1–93

Hudgins, C. and Numbers, F. (1942) An investigation of the intelligibility of the speech of the deaf. *Genetic Psychology* 25, 289–392

Huntington, A. and Watton, F. (1984a). Language and interaction in the education of hearing-impaired children, (Part 1). *Journal of the British Association of Teachers of the Deaf* 8, 4, 109–117

Huntington, A. and Watton, F. (1984b). Language and interaction in the education of hearing-impaired children, (Part 2). *Journal of the British Association of Teachers of the Deaf* 8, 5, 137–144

Ivimey, G. (1977) The perception of speech: an information-processing approach. Part 2 – perceptual and cognitive processes. *Journal of the British Association of Teachers of the Deaf* 1, 64–73

Ivimey, G. (1981) The psychological bases of oral education. In Mulholland, A. (ed.) *Oral Education Today and Tomorrow*. Washington, DC: A.G. Bell Association

Ivimey, G. and Lachterman, D. (1980) The written language of young English deaf children. *Language and Speech* Part 4, 23, 351–377

John, J. and Howarth, J. (1965) The effect of time distortions on the intelligibility of deaf children's speech. *Language and Speech* 8, 127–134

Johnson, R.E. and Erting, C. (1989) Ethnicity and socialization in a classroom for deaf children. In Lucas, C. (ed.) *The Sociolinguistics of the Deaf Community*. San Diego: Academic Press

Johnson, R.E., Liddell, S.K. and Erting, C.J. (1989) Unlocking the curriculum: principles for achieving access in deaf education. Gallaudet Research Institute Working Paper 89-3. Washington, DC: Gallaudet University

Johnson, R.C. (1990) The publication and early aftermath of unlocking the curriculum. *Sign Language Studies* 69, 295–325

Jordan, I. (1982) Communication methods used at schools for deaf and partially hearing children and at units for partially hearing children in the United Kingdom. *American Annals of the Deaf* 127, 7, 811–815

Kannapell, B. (1989) An examination of deaf college students' attitudes toward ASL and English. In Lucas, C. (ed.) *The Sociolinguistics of the Deaf Community*. London: Academic Press

Kettlety, A. (1975) New National Health Service hearing aids for children. *The Teacher of the Deaf* **73**, 200–207

Kluwin, T. (1981) A rationale for modifying classroom signing systems. *Sign Language Studies* **31**, 179–187

Kretschmer, R. and Kretschmer, L. (1978). *Language Development and Interaction with the Hearing Impaired*. Baltimore: University Park Press

Kyle, J. and Ackerman, J. (1990) Assessing BSL competence in deaf children in Total Communication programmes. Rochester, NY: International Congress on Education of the Deaf

Kyle, J. and Woll, B. (1985) *Sign Language: the Study of Deaf People and their Language*. Cambridge: Cambridge University Press

Ladd, P. (1981) The erosion of social and self identity. In Montgomery. G. (ed.) *The Integration and Disintegration of the Deaf in Society*. Scottish Workshop Publications

Ladd, P. (1988) Hearing-impaired or British Sign Language users? Social policies and the deaf community. *Disability, Handicap and Society*, **3**, 2, 195–199

Lai, M. and Lynas, W. (1991) Communication mode and interaction style. *Child Language Teaching and Therapy* **7**, 3, 239–259

Latimer, G. (1983) TC or not TC? – That is the question. *Journal of the British Association of Teachers of the Deaf* **7**, 4, 99–101

Lawson, L. (1981) Integration? Personal experience. In Montgomery. G. (ed) *The Integration and Disintegration of the Deaf in Society*. Scottish Workshop Publications

Levine, E. (1976) Psychological determinants in personality development. *Volta Review* **78**, 258–267

Lewis, S. (1994) The reading achievements of a group of hearing-impaired school leavers. *Journal of the British Association of Teachers of the Deaf* (in press)

Lewis, S. and Richards, S. (1988) The early stages of language development: a natural aural approach. *Journal of the British Association of Teachers of the Deaf* **12**, 2, 33–38

Lindahl, U. and Andersson, R. (1990) Deaf teachers in the bilingual education of the deaf in Sweden. Rochester, NY: International Congress on Education of the Deaf.

Ling, D. and Ling, A. (1978) *Aural Habilitation*. Washington, DC: A.G. Bell Association

Livingstone, S. (1983) Levels of development in the language of deaf children. *Sign Language Studies* **40**, 193–286

Lucas, C. (1989) *The Sociolinguistics of the Deaf Community*. London: Academic Press

Lynas, W. (1986) *Integrating the Handicapped into Ordinary Schools: A Study of Hearing-Impaired Pupils*. London: Croom Helm

Lynas, W., Huntington, A. and Tucker, I. (1988) *A Critical Examination of Different Approaches to Communication in the Education of Deaf Children*. The Ewing Foundation

Maestas Y. and Moores, J. (1980). Early language environment: interactions of deaf parents with their infants. *Sign Language Studies* **26**, 1–13

Mallery-Ruganis, D., Wilkins, D. and Fischer, S. (1990) Implications of Research for the Teaching of Simultaneous Communication. Rochester, NY: NTID

Markides, A. (1986) Age at fitting of hearing aids and speech intelligibility. *British Journal of Audiology* **20**, 165–168

Markides, A. (1988) Speech intelligibility: auditory-oral approach versus total communication. *Journal of the British Association of Teachers of the Deaf* **12**, 6, 136–141

Markowicz, H. (1990) Interview. In Johnson, R.C. On unlocking the curriculum. *Sign Language Studies* **69**, 295–325

Markowicz, H. and Woodward, J. (1978) Language and the maintenance of ethnic boundaries in the deaf community. *Communication and Cognition* **11**, 29–38

Marmor. G. and Petitto, L. (1979) Simultaneous communication in the classroom: how well is English grammar represented? In Stokoe, W. (ed.) *Sign Language Studies*, Silver Spring, MD: Linstock Press

Martin, M. and Lodge, J. (1969) A survey of hearing aids in schools for the deaf and partially hearing units. *Sound* **3**, 2–11

Mason, C. (1990) Cited in *British Deaf News* p. 6. Carlisle: British Deaf Association

Matthews, T. and Reich, C. (1993) Constraints on communication in classrooms for the deaf. *American Annals of the Deaf* **138**, 1, 14–18

Maxwell, M. (1985) Sign language instruction and teacher preparation. *Sign Language Studies* **47**, 173–180

Maxwell, M. (1990) Simultaneous communication: the state of the art and proposals for change. *Sign Language Studies* **69**, 333–390

McAnally, P., Rose, S. and Quigley, S. (1987) *Language Learning Practices with Deaf Children*. Boston: College-Hill Press

Meadow, K. (1968) Early manual communication in relation to the deaf child's intellectual, social and communicative functioning. *American Annals of the Deaf* **113**, 29–41

Meadow, K. (1980) *Deafness and Child Development*. London: Edward Arnold

Merrill, E. (1976) *Universal Rights and Progress in Education of the Deaf*. Carlisle: British Deaf Association

Merrill, E. (1981) Normalisation or integration? The role of deaf people in education and society. In Montgomery, G. (ed.) *The Integration and Disintegration of the Deaf in Society*. Scottish Workshop Publications

Miles, D. (1988) *British Sign Language: A Beginner's Guide*. London: BBC Books (The book accompanies the BBC video, first broadcast BBC1 Spring, 1988.)

Mills, A.E. and Coerts, J. (1990) Function and forms of bilingual input: children learning a sign language as one of their first languages. In Prillevitz, S. and Vellhaber, T. (eds) *Current Trends in European Sign Language Research*. Hamburg: Signum

Mitchell, G. (1984) *Total Communication in the 80s: An Overview*. Proceedings of the Sign 84 Conference, Edinburgh

Mogford, K. and Bishop, J. (1988) Five questions about language acquisition considered in the light of exceptional circumstances. In Bishop, J. and Mogford, K. (eds) *Language Development in Exceptional Circumstances*. London: Churchill Livingstone

Montgomery, G. (1980) *Effective Brains vs Defective Ears*. Carlisle: British Deaf Association

Moodley, A. (1989) Acoustic conditions in mainstream classrooms. *Journal of the British Association of Teachers of the Deaf* **13**, 2, 48–54

Moog, J. (1988) Cited in: Deaf education debate: signing vs. the spoken word. *Medical Record* **12**, 34

Moores, D. (1992) Editorial. *American Annals of the Deaf* **137**, 4, 307

Mottez, B. (1990) Deaf identity. *Sign Language Studies* 68, 195–216

Myklebust, H. (1964) *The Psychology of Deafness*. New York: Grune & Stratton

National Aural Group (1981) Promoting natural language through residual hearing. *Journal of the British Association of Teachers of the Deaf* 5, 3, Magazine Section

Newell, A. and Simon, H. (1972) *Human Problem Solving*. Englewood Cliffs, NJ: Prentice-Hall

Newton, L. (1985) Linguistic environment of the deaf child: a focus on teachers' use of non-literal language. *Journal of Speech and Hearing Research* 28, 336–364

Nix, G. (1981) The right to be heard. *Volta Review* 83, 199–205

Nolan, M. and Tucker, I. (1988) *The Hearing-Impaired Child and the Family*. London: Souvenir Press, second edition

Norden, K. (1981) Learning processes and personality development in deaf children. *American Annals of the Deaf* 126, 404–410

Northcott, W. (1981) Freedom through speech: every child's right. *Volta Review* 83, 3, 162–181

O'Rourke, T. (1990) Teaching English to deaf students and English as a second language: psychological considerations. An academic panel discussion moderated by Terence O'Rourke. Panellists: Kathee Christensen, Astrid Goodstein, Tom Humphries, Marlon Kuntze, Anne Titus, Michael Strong. *Teaching English to Deaf and Second-Language Students* 8, 1, 5–19

Ogden, P. (1982) Cited in Arnold, P. and Francis, E. Deaf people's views of speech and signing. *Journal of the British Association of Teachers of the Deaf* 7, 3, 58–9

Oliver, M. (1990) *The Politics of Disablement*. London: Macmillan

Padden, C. and Humphries, T. (1988) *Deaf in America: Voices from a Culture*. Cambridge: Harvard University Press

Parasnis, I. (1983) Effects of parental deafness on early exposure to manual communication on the cognitive skills, English language skills and field independence of young deaf adults. *Journal of Speech and Hearing Research* 26, 588–594

Paul, P. (1987) A perspective on using American Sign Language to teach English as a second language. *Teaching English to Deaf and Second-Language Students* 5, 3, 10–16

Paul, P. (1988) American Sign Language and English: A bi-lingual minority language immersion program. *CAID — News'N'Notes*. Washington, DC: Conference of American Instructors of the Deaf

Paul, P. and Quigley, S. (1990) *Education and Deafness*. New York: Longman

Petitto, L. (1987) On the autonomy of language and gesture: evidence from the acquisition of personal pronouns in American Sign Language. *Cognition* 27, 1–52

Petitto, L. (1988) 'Language' in the pre-linguistic child. In Chesses, F. (ed) *The Development of Language and Language Researchers*. Hillsdale, NJ: Erlbaum

Pickersgill, M. (1990a). Bilingualism and the education of deaf children: Part 1. Theories, models and factors. *Deafness and Development* 1, 1, 10–14

Pickersgill, M. (1990b) Bilingualism and the education of deaf children: Part 2. Implications and practical considerations. *Deafness and Development* 1, 2, 3–8

Pickersgill, M. (1991) Bilingualism and the education of deaf children: Part 3. Towards a model of good practice. *Deafness and Development* 2, 1, 4–9

Potts, G. (1974) Some impressions of the services for the hearing impaired in

Denmark. *Teachers of the Deaf* 72, 244–250

Powers, S. (1990) A survey of secondary units for hearing-impaired children, Part 1. *Journal of the British Association of Teachers of the Deaf* 14, 3, 69–79

Quigley, S. and Kretschmer, R. (1982) *The Education of Deaf Children: Issues, Theory and Practice*. London: Arnold

Quigley, S. and Frisina, D. (1961) Institutionalisation and Psycho-educational Development of Deaf Children. Council for Exceptional Children Research Monograph (Series A, No. 3)

Quigley, S. and Paul, P. (1984) *Language and Deafness*. San Diego: Singular Publishing Group

Ramsey, C. (1990) Classroom discourse and literacy learning in an elementary school mainstreaming programme for deaf students. Rochester, NY: International Congress on the Education of the Deaf

Reid, C. (1991) Education for life? In Taylor, G. and Bishop, J. (eds) *Being Deaf: The Experience of Deafness*. London: Open University

Ritter-Brinton, K. (1990) Signed English and the hearing family. International Congress on Education of the Deaf, Rochester, NY

Robinshaw, H. (1992) Communication and language development in deaf and hearing infants. Unpublished Ph.D thesis, University of Cambridge

Royal School for the Deaf (1989) Policy Statement. Ashbourne Road, Derby DE3 3BH

Sacks, O. (1989) *Seeing Voices*. London: Pan Books

Schaper, M. and Reitsma, P. (1993) The use of speech-based recoding in reading by prelingually deaf children. *American Annals of the Deaf* 138, 1, 46–54

Schildroth, A. and Hotto, S. (1991) Annual survey of hearing impaired children and youth: 1989–90 school year. *American Annals of the Deaf* 136, 2, 155–164

Schlesinger, H. (1986) Total Communication in Perspective. In Luterman, D. (ed.) *Deafness in Perspective*. London: Taylor & Francis

Schlesinger, H. and Meadow, K. (1972) *Sound and Sign: Childhood Deafness and Mental Health*, Berkeley: University of California Press

Simpson, P., Harrison, D. and Stuart, A. (1992) The reading abilities of a population of hearing-impaired children. *Journal of the British Association of Teachers of the Deaf* 16, 2, 47–52

Smith, C. (1990) *Signs Make Sense*. London: Souvenir Press

Snow, C. (1977) The development of conversation between mothers and babies. *Journal of Child Language* 4, 1–22

Staab, W. (1990) Digital/programmable hearing aids — an eye towards the future. *British Journal of Audiology* 24, 243–256

Stewart, D. (1990) Directions in bilingual education for deaf children. *Teaching English to Deaf and Second-Language Students* 8, 2, 4–9

Stokes, J. and Bamford, J. (1990) Transition from pre-linguistic to linguistic communication in hearing-impaired infants. *British Journal of Audiology* 24, 217–222

Stokoe, W. (1960) *Sign Language Structure*. Silver Spring: Linstock Press

Stone, P. and Adam, A. (1986) Is your child wearing the right hearing aid? Principles for selecting and maintaining amplification. *Volta Review* 88, 5, 45–54

Strong, M. and Charlson, E. (1987) Simultaneous communication: how teachers approach an impossible task. *American Annals of the Deaf* 132, 376–382

Strong, M., Woodward, J. and Burdett, J. (1987) A bilingual/ESL approach to the education of deaf children. *Teaching English to Deaf and Second-Language*

Students 5, 1, 8–20

Stuckless, E. and Birch, J. (1966) The influence of early manual communication on the linguistic development of deaf children. *American Annals of the Deaf* 113, 29–41

Sutherland, A. (1981) *Disabled We Stand*. London: Souvenir Press

Suty, K.A. and Friel-Patty, S. (1982) Looking beyond sign language to describe the language of two deaf children. *Sign Language Studies* 35, 153–168

Swift Parrino, S. (1990) Opening address. International Congress on Education of the Deaf, Rochester, NY

Swisher, M. (1990) Conversational interaction between deaf children and their mothers: the role of visual attention. In Siple, P. and Fischer, S. (eds) *Theoretical Issues in Sign Language Research: Psychology*. Chicago: University of Chicago Press

Tervoort, B. (1961) Esoteric symbolism in the communication behavior of young deaf children. *American Annals of the Deaf* 106, 436–438

Thompson, M. and Swisher, M. (1985) Acquiring language through total communication. *Ear and Hearing* 6, 29–32

Tough, J. (1977) *The Development of Meaning*. London: Allen & Unwin

Treesburg, J. (1990) TBC News, Feb 1990, No. 22. Riverdale, MD: The Bicultural Centre

Trotter, J. (1989) An examination of language attitudes of teachers of the deaf. In Lucas, C. (ed) *The Sociolinguistics of the Deaf Community*. London: Academic Press

Tucker, I. (1986) Some aspects of the verbal and non-verbal interaction of parents and their hearing-impaired children. Unpublished doctoral thesis, University of Manchester

Tucker, I. and Powell, C. (1991) *The Hearing-Impaired Child and School*. London: Souvenir Press

Tumim, W. (1982) Intonation as a clue to first language learning in hearing-impaired children. Paper to the British Society of Audiology and College of Speech Therapists. London

Van Uden, A. (1977) *A World of Language for Deaf Children, Part 1. Basic Principles*. Amsterdam: Swets and Zeitlinger

Van Uden, A. (1986) *Sign Languages Used by Deaf People and Psycholinguistics: A Critical Evaluation*. Lisse: Swets and Zeitlinger

Watson, T. (1967) *The Education of Hearing-Handicapped Children*. London: University of London Press

Weisel, A., Dromi, E. and Dor, S. (1990) Exploration of factors affecting attitudes towards sign language. *Sign Language Studies* 68, 257–276

Wells, G. (1981) *Learning Through Interaction: The Study of Language Development*. Cambridge: Cambridge University Press

Wells, G. (1986) *Language Development in the Pre-School Years*. Cambridge: Cambridge University Press

White, A. and Stevenson, V. (1975) The effects of Total Communication, manual communication, oral communication and reading on the learning of factual information in residential school deaf children. *American Annals of the Deaf* 120, 48–57

Williams, P. (1982) *We Can Speak for Ourselves*. London: Souvenir Press

Winston, E. (1990) English use in the Deaf community. Rochester, NY: International Congress of the Education of the Deaf

Wolk, S. and Schildroth, A. (1986) Deaf children and speech intelligibility: a national study. In Schildroth, A. and Karchmer, M. (eds) *Deaf Children in America*. San Diego: College-Hill Press

Woll, B. and Kyle, J. (1989) Communication and language development in children of deaf parents. In von Tetzchner, S., Siegel, L. and Smith, L. (eds) *The Social and Cognitive Aspects of Normal and Atypical Language Development*. New York: Springer Verlag

Wood, D. and Wood, H. (1992a) Signed English in the classroom, III. What gets signed? *First Language* 12, 1–15

Wood, D. and Wood, H. (1992b) Signed English in the classroom, IV. Aspects of children's speech and sign. *First Language* 12, 125–145

Wood, D., Wood, H., Griffiths, A. and Howarth, I. (1986) *Teaching and Talking with Deaf Children*. Chichester: John Wiley

Woodward, J. (1982). *How You Gonna Get to Heaven if You Can't Talk with Jesus: On Depathologising Deafness*. Silver Spring, MD: T.J. Publishers

Woodward, J., Allen, T. and Schildroth, A. (1987) English teachers of the deaf: background and communication preferences. *Teaching English to Deaf and Second-Language Students* 5, 2, 4–13

Index